Showing Dogs

Showing Dogs

The Exhibitors' Guide

JULIETTE CUNLIFFE

All photographs are by Carol Ann Johnson, unless otherwise stated

First published in the UK in 2007 by Swan Hill Press, an imprint of Quiller Publishing Ltd

British Library Cataloguing-in-Publication Data
A catalogue record for this book is available from the British Library

ISBN 978 1 84689 002 4

Printed in China

Swan Hill Press
An imprint of Quiller Publishing Ltd
Wykey House, Wykey, Shrewsbury, SY4 1JA
Tel: 01939 261616 Fax: 01939 261606
E-mail: info@quillerbooks.com
Website: www.countrybooksdirect.com

CONTENTS

A hot day at a summer Championship Show. Note the dog wearing a heat repelling coat. (CUNLIFFE)

CHAPTER 1

DO YOU REALLY WANT TO SHOW?

Dog showing can be enormous fun, an opportunity to meet other like-minded folk and to have an enjoyable day out with your dog. However, it's not all plain sailing. As a dog show enthusiast you will encounter many 'ups and downs' along the way. In this book I hope to give you an insight into the dog show world and to help alleviate some of the difficulties you may encounter so that, with luck, you will have more 'ups' than 'downs'.

Firstly perhaps I should explain that the dog show world is much bigger than most people imagine, unless of course they are involved from the inside, as you probably plan to be. In Britain there can be well over 20,000 dogs at a Championship Show, which is usually spread over three or four days. In addition there are at least as many people at a show, sometimes even twice as many when one takes into account exhibitors, handlers and visitors. Most shows have plenty of food stalls and trade stands, so you can see that, all in all, it is a veritable hive of activity. Dog shows in other countries can be just as busy and full of activity, but the number of dogs shown rarely meets the number we see in the UK.

Of course there are many smaller shows too, and it is probably best to begin showing your first dog at these, so later we shall discuss the various different types of show that you might like to consider.

The quality of your dog will most probably be the deciding factor as to which type of show you enter, or if indeed you enter at all. You may have selected your very first show dog with competition in mind, so you will hopefully have obtained a good quality dog from a reputable breeder who has sold you something that has suitable potential for exhibition. However, even the most experienced and dedicated breeder can never be absolutely certain that the puppy they sell at eight or ten weeks old will turn out quite as expected. Also, the way the new owner cares for and trains the puppy will have considerable bearing on the likelihood of achieving success in the showring.

Many people get into showing by having a pedigree pet dog that they have been told looks well-worthy of showing. Provided they have all the required Kennel Club documentation for the dog there is nothing to prevent them from doing so and indeed they may have a lot of fun at shows, particularly at smaller ones where the competition is not particularly strong in some of the classes. However, most people who start this way, sooner or later realise that they are never likely to do any really top winning and so they go on to purchase another dog that they have selected specifically with the showring in mind. Of course there are exceptions, but dogs bought as pets are far less likely to achieve top honours in the ring.

A well organised Open Show held outdoors, with a combination of tented and open-air accommodation for dogs and exhibitors. (CUNLIFFE)

All the activity of a Show.

Do you have the time and the money?

Showing a dog is both a time consuming and a costly hobby, at least when competing at high level. Let us look first of all at the time involved, which will vary to a certain extent depending upon what kind of breed you have decided to show.

A smooth-coated breed will clearly not take up much of your time when it comes to coat care, but still some time must be set aside because skin and coat must be maintained in good condition; your dog will probably need the occasional bath and nails must be kept in trim, ears checked and teeth kept clean. If yours is a long-coated breed the time involved in keeping the coat in tip-top condition will be considerably greater, and neither you should not be deceived into thinking that one of the smart looking, short-coated Terrier breeds involves no work. It does! Keeping many of the Terrier breeds in show condition is a dedicated task and involves a considerable amount of work and skill on the part of the owner. In short, if you plan to show your dog, you must be prepared to care for its coat yourself. Don't be fooled into thinking that you will take your dog along to a professional grooming parlour from time to time; that may be an option for the pet owner, but not for a show exhibitor.

The whole family celebrates a wonderful Best in Show win for this Welsh Terrier.

Exercising your dog will also take up your time, but this is sure to be very enjoyable. The tiny Toy breeds may indeed get as much exercise as they need in and around your home and garden, but the larger breeds will need time devoted to road work as well as free exercise if their muscles are to be kept in peak condition. The amount of exercise and the form it should take will depend not only on the size of dog, but also on the breed. For example some of the very large breeds, such as the Great Dane, Irish Wolfhound and Deerhound, should not have much controlled exercise at all during the crucial period of bone growth, and yet when

These three young lads were proud to show off the Great Danes belonging to their uncle.

fully mature they will need plenty. If you have bought your dog from an experienced breeder you should already have received sound advice as to what amount of exercise is suitable for your particular breed, and when it should be given.

Dog showing is by no means an inexpensive hobby, nor indeed is dog ownership. If you own any dog, you should be certain that you have sufficient means to care for your dog well, which means feeding a good quality diet and being able to afford veterinary bills whenever they might arise. If you have only one, two or perhaps three dogs it may well be cost-effective to take out a veterinary insurance policy, so that vet's bills are covered, for these can mount up enormously if ever there is a crisis or serious illness. But even if you have an insurance policy for your dog, you will still have to pay for any routine vaccinations that may be necessary.

In addition if you are going to show your dog, you will need to spend money on

Smiles all round for exhibitor and judge, this Miniature Schnauzer having just been awarded Best Puppy in Group at a Championship Show.

grooming equipment and if you have a small dog you will need a grooming table and possibly a trolley. Long-coated dogs will usually need a special canine hairdryer, so although these will be purchases that will last you many years, there is still a hefty financial outlay at the outset.

Then you will have to consider the actual cost of attending shows. Not only will there be the cost of fuel, which seems to be ever on the increase, but the cost of show entries can be considerable. The genuine dog show enthusiast travels many miles to reach Championship Shows, sometimes even from Scotland to the south coast, or vice versa. And, by the way, is your current car large enough to transport your dogs in comfort, or might you need to change to something larger or more practical?

At Championship Shows the cost is usually over £20 to enter one dog in one class, with about £3 per entry in any additional class with the same dog. Take two dogs to a show and you've doubled that; take three and it's trebled. Breed specific Championship Shows usually cost somewhat less at around £8 to £12 per entry and Open Show entries are much less again. For those of you who just want to have fun at local Companion Dog Shows, the entry fees are usually only £1 or £2 and those you attend will usually be in your own local area.

In addition to entry fees, you will most probably also want to purchase a show schedule, which will generally cost £4 to £6 at a big show, and if you are not the sort of practical person who takes along a picnic lunch, you will need to buy your own food and refreshments at the show, further pushing up the expense of showing.

Well, I hope I have not put you off so far, but I feel it only fair to point out that dog showing can easily burn a hole in your pocket, just like many other hobbies.

Making friends, and maybe enemies too

Dog shows offer an ideal opportunity to make new friends. Everyone knows that if you walk a dog in the park there is an increased opportunity of getting into conversation with someone. The dog provides a focal point, something to smile at, speak to, or perhaps fondle. So it is at dog shows.

However large or small the show, you are sure to come across other dog owners who are happy to talk to you, and if you are a newcomer to the dog showing world, perhaps to offer advice. As time goes on, you will decide for yourself whether the advice you are offered is sound or otherwise. Dog showing seems to be one of those hobbies in which people who have been involved for 'five minutes' are overly happy to offer their profound advice and reasoning to the really raw newcomer. Such advice is not always well founded, though frequently well meant.

There are sure to be people with whom you become friendly over time, though at large Championship Shows there is every chance that the people you meet don't live in your own area. Exhibitors generally travel less distance to Open Shows, so if you exhibit at local Open Shows, you may well find friends who live fairly near and maybe you will even decide to travel with them to shows that are further away.

Don't be surprised, though, that if you are fortunate enough to do some considerable winning with your dog, other dog folk become rather jealous. Very jealous indeed sometimes. The people who used to sit beside you and offer advice, are probably less willing to do so now that your dog has beaten theirs a few times. But this is the way of the 'dog game' and you will soon come to realise which people are the ones you can truly count on as friends. They will be happy for you when you win and will share in the pleasure you derive from your success.

Coping with pleasure and disappointment

If you win you are sure to be pleased, but try to avoid boasting about it too much, and of course you should always remember to congratulate the winners who stand ahead of you in the final line up. Hopefully they will also congratulate you when it is your turn to win a first prize.

Inevitably there are what are known as good and bad losers at dog shows, so even if you are not happy with your placing, or perhaps you have not won an award at all, try not to show your disappointment in the ring. Remember that every judge will have a slightly different opinion as to what constitutes a good show dog in your breed, so on another occasion, under a different judge and against different competition, you may have more success.

This American Cocker Spaniel was Britain's Top Dog All Breeds in 2005.

Is your dog really good enough to win at shows?

Dog showing is a highly competitive sport, and there are some really experienced people out there, expertly preparing and handling top quality dogs. This means that if you want to have any chance of winning at high level, you must have a very good specimen of your breed to take into the ring.

In fairness to yourself, you must be honest about the merits of your own dog. It's all too easy to be 'kennel blind' and to overlook even the most obvious faults. Unless you are extremely fortunate, the chances are that your first show dog will be one with which you learn the ropes, so to speak. You may do some moderate winning in the lower classes and this will give you great pleasure. When you first start out, you will probably be delighted to receive a fifth prize in a class of six, but those of us who have been in the game a good while would probably be secretly devastated!

The big difference is that those who have been showing dogs for decades have learned the ropes and probably have an in-depth knowledge of the breed, so they know whether or not the dog is truly worthy of exhibiting. There is no perfect dog, but an experienced owner will know the dog's faults and will know how to disguise them as far as possible. This same exhibitor will also, in all probability, know which judges are likely to appreciate his dog's merits and will therefore not enter under those judges who are less likely to do so. Although it is every judge's duty to compare dogs against the Kennel Club breed standard, there is always some element of personal preference involved. If there were not, the same dogs would win at every show, which is certainly not the case at all.

Can I handle and present my dog sufficiently well?

Never lose sight of the fact that during your first few years in the showring you are a relative newcomer. You will hopefully start learning from day one, but if you are a truly dedicated exhibitor you will recognise that you will continue to learn throughout your life in the world of dogs. Things in the dog world are ever changing. Grooming products and the presentation of dogs has come on in leaps and bounds over the last few decades. One has only to look back at the way coated dogs were presented in the middle of the last century to see how 'finished' the show dog looks now in comparison. And if you look back a full century or more your eyes will probably pop out of your head!

If you want to achieve success with your dog in the showring, you will need to learn how best to present your exhibit. You may have been able to pick some tips from your local ringcraft class, but more importantly you will have watched other, more experienced exhibitors very carefully. You may not agree with everything they do, but the more you watch, listen and learn, the better position you will be in to sieve out the little snippets that will help you with your own dog.

Look carefully at the grooming equipment people use on their dogs. What seems to produce the best results in your own breed? How much or how little do other people exercise their dogs before entering the ring? This may depend on your dog's personality, so will have to be very carefully considered. An owner with a long-coated breed will not exercise it in the rain at a show or it will enter the ring looking like a drowned rat, so don't make that mistake with your own dog or you will stand no chance at all of standing at the front of the line when the judge makes his awards.

Look, too, at the way experienced exhibitors present their dogs in the ring. See what tips you can pick up that may enhance the way you can present your own dog. Obviously, initially you will learn most from watching your own breed being judged, but you can also learn a great deal from watching exhibitors of other breeds too.

So, if you have decided to seriously show your dog you will have a lot of work ahead of you. Showing is sure to be enjoyable, but there will be bad days too when nothing seems to go right; perhaps your dog doesn't behave well, the judge just doesn't seem to appreciate the 'type' of dog you have, or maybe it's poured with rain all day and dog showing just doesn't seem much fun at all. Look on the bright side; there's always another show to go to and if you are really meant to be a dog show person you will somehow overcome all obstacles that stand in your way.

Many exhibitors use mobile homes, this one aptly named 'The Sheltie Shuttle'.

Combining dog showing with caravanning

Although the majority of exhibitors travel to shows just for the day, many people make a holiday of it by taking their caravan along and spending several days away. This is well worth considering if you already own a caravan or motor home, or perhaps are considering buying one.

There is great camaraderie amongst the caravan fraternity and most general championship shows have special caravan areas set aside for dog exhibitors. The caravan parks rarely have all the mod cons that one might expect on a permanent caravan site, but often loos and showers are available, the latter sometimes at restricted times, if your own van doesn't have these facilities. At some shows the number of caravan spaces is limited, so

Everything seems possible when caravanning at a dog show. This exhibitor is bathing his dog outside his caravan in preparation for the show the following day.

you will need to book well in advance. This can usually be done when you submit your dog's entry form for the show. There is of course a fee to be paid and although this varies from show to show, the price is rarely too exorbitant.

Dog show caravan parks are very special because they, understandably, house so many dogs. All sorts of contraptions are set up around the caravans, with awnings and safety barriers so that people's dogs can be housed in safety and comfort. But do please make sure that you keep a careful check on the dogs in your caravan area, always remembering that heat can build up very quickly and that heatstroke can affect dogs anywhere, not just inside cars.

People who stay at shows in caravans usually take all their dogs along with them, which means that a dog-sitter is not needed to look after the non-show dogs at home. It also has the added advantage that if you are exhibiting different breeds, due to be shown on different days, you do not have to traipse all the way home to change over your dogs, possibly having to bath one or more dogs in the middle of the night before setting off again early the next day.

Some exhibitors have all their grooming equipment set up with their caravans, so that dogs can be bathed and dried with a professional dryer so that they look their very best on show day. If you plan to do this is it is necessary to have a generator, since caravan sites on show grounds are temporary affairs and there are no power supplies to which one can hook up.

On sunny evenings dog show people do all the things that other caravanners do, with barbecues galore and lots of social activities. At least one show even organises a fancy dress party on the showground, which is a regular feature year after year.

Especially during the summer season, the major championship shows run on from each other so rapidly that there is often only a gap of two or three days between shows. Because of this many people simply move from one show to another, often for weeks on end and, because everyone these days has mobile phones and in many cases laptop computers, there is still plenty of chance to keep in touch with the outside world.

Things to Think About

How much time will be involved?

What will dog showing cost?

Can I cope with the disappointment?

What kind of dog would I like to show?

Is my dog good enough to win?

Can I handle my dog well enough?

Might I enjoy caravanning at shows?

These Weimeraners won the Breeder's Team at Crufts under judge Claire Coxall.

CHAPTER 2

GETTING PREPARED

It's all well and good deciding that you want to show your dog, but of course you will have to find out which shows are about to take place and where they are. You may also decide to take your dog along to ringcraft classes initially, just to get to know the ropes, so let's begin there.

Ringcraft

In most towns and some villages ringcraft classes are held, often hosted by the local dog show society. They usually take place one evening each week and provide an opportunity to practise with your dog in a semi-show environment, before entering the showring proper. Ringcraft classes are also often used by experienced exhibitors who need to practise with a new puppy, or perhaps they have an older dog that has for some reason gone a little 'ring shy' and needs to regain its confidence.

You will probably be able to find details of a local ringcraft class from your vet's, for the chances are that someone involved either uses the vet or has told them about it, or perhaps posted a notice on the board. Another avenue is to telephone the Kennel Club and to ask for telephone contact details of the various dog clubs in your area. By phoning these you are almost certain to obtain the information you need.

If you live in a very remote rural area, you may have to travel some distance to a local training class, but there is usually one within about a twenty mile radius. In towns there is often much more selection, and if this is the case you will be in the fortunate position of being able to choose the one that suits you best, not just from the point of view of convenience, but also of quality. Some ringcraft classes are much better run than others, and you should always keep in the back of your mind that the people who assess the dogs are not always highly experienced themselves. Often they are, but there is no rule of thumb and such classes are often used as training ground for prospective judges who are still on the first rung of the ladder.

Therefore when you have located such a class, I would suggest that for your first visit you just go along to watch, ideally without your dog. However, if your dog is fully vaccinated and able to go out and about in public, you may decide to take him along too, but remember that this first introduction to the canine world at large can be a little overpowering for a youngster, so you would be well advised just to let him sit on your lap for a while, or if he is too big for that, find a spot where he can sit quietly by your side to

Before taking your youngster to its first show, it is sensible to practise getting the dog's movement just right, as this exhibitor is doing in a quiet lane with her Alaskan Malamute puppy.

watch what is going on and absorb the atmosphere. I should perhaps point out that finding a quiet spot at a ringcraft class is not always possible, especially if the venue is small and everyone has decided to take a dog along for practise that night!

In the early stages it is best to attend classes every week, but usually there is no set term, except at privately run training organisations. This means that people and dogs come and go, so you will not always meet the same people and dogs each week. Some ringcraft classes divide the dogs up into classes, according usually to age. If this is the case, this may determine the time at which you need to arrive, so check this out with the organisers before going along.

Usually the weekly fee to attend a ringcraft class hosted by a local dog club is very reasonable, so you and your dog can spend a pleasant evening in good company, even with a cup of tea and a biscuit, for very little money. There will most probably also be an annual joining fee but this, too, will be minimal.

The idea of a ringcraft class is to give dogs practice for an actual show, so you will be asked to stand your dog in a show pose at the side of the ring, following which he will be assessed either on the floor or on a table depending on his size. Then you will be asked to move your dog up and down a non-slip mat which will have been taken along especially for the purpose, or if the venue is large enough you may be asked to move in a triangle. By no means every owner at ringcraft class has experience in the showring, so may not have the ability to control their dog as well as might be expected. Therefore keep your wits about you with your own new recruit so that no accidents happen such as a dog attacking your puppy, for this would probably set him back and make him reluctant to show with confidence in the future.

Finding out about shows

Judge Meriel Hathaway has selected these two Keeshonds as winners of the Brace competition.

To find out about all dog shows you will need to subscribe to one of the weekly canine newspapers, which in the UK are *Our Dogs* and *Dog World*. Although you may be able to buy these at large newsagents in major cities, to avoid disappointment you should really place a regular order, either with your newsagent or directly with the papers themselves, in which case each issue will arrive by post, usually on a Friday.

All show societies advertise their forthcoming shows via this media and this is the only certain way of finding out about them all. Each show advertisement will include a telephone number so that you will be able to contact the show secretary and ask for a schedule to be posted to you. A relatively recent innovation is that some societies now offer the facility of downloading the show schedule and entry form from the internet, and in some cases it is even possible to enter on-line, usually with a slightly later deadline.

Those exhibitors who have entered at a society's show will usually automatically be sent a schedule through the post for the next event, but it is still wise to keep your eyes peeled for press announcements so there is no chance of it being overlooked.

Another reminder of show dates and the dates by which entries must be submitted is to be found in the dog diaries offered for sale towards the close of each year. However, please bear in mind that occasionally it is necessary for a show society to change the date of a show so these diaries may have been printed before the change was announced. Hence it is essential that you double check to avoid missing any changes that may have been made.

Entries for shows close well in advance, sometimes as long as eight weeks prior. The timescale is shorter for Open Shows and usually for Breed Club Shows, though it is still generally about a month beforehand.

MIDLAND COUNTIES CANIN
31st BENCHED GENERAL CHAMPIONSH
(Judged on the Group System) (held under Kennel Club Rules
Thursday, 26th October 20
Friday, 27th October 2006
Saturday, 28th October 200
Sunday, 29th October 2006
The New Bingley Hall, Count
ENTRIES CLOSE: Tuesday, 12th SEPTEM
ON-LINE ENTRIES CLOSE: Tuesday, 19
Enter on-line at www.fossedata.net
YOU MAY ENTER ALL YOUR BREEDS ON ONE ENTRY FORM.
PLEASE USE A SEPARATE FORM FOR EACH OWNER
REGISTERED NAME OF DOG
(and ATC Number if applicable)
KC ATC No.
KC ATC No.
KC ATC No.
KC ATC No.
DECLARATION
Fosse Data Systems Ltd., Newton, Rugby, Warwickshire CV23 0TB.

I/we enclose cheque/P.O. to cover the following:
DISABLED CAR PARK
Please indicate (see Page 12)
Switch
Delta
Postcode:
Dam
Letters Please)
To be entered in classes
(MR/MRS/MISS/MS)
TEL (STD)

Midland Counties Canine Society
SCHEDULE OF 31st Championship Dog Show
Held under Kennel Club Rules & Regulations on Group System of Judging
Thursday, 26th October 2006
Gundog
Friday, 27th October 2006
Pastoral & Working
Saturday, 28th October 2006
Toy & Utility
Sunday, 29th October 2006
Hound & Terrier
at
The New Bingley Hall
County Showground
Stafford ST18 0BD
Entries Close:
TUESDAY, 12th SEPTEMBER 2006
on-line entries close: 19th September
Secretary:
Mrs Margaret Everton,
Ashram, Pickersleigh Road,
Malvern Link, Worcs WR14 2RS
Tel: 01684 572375
(9.00am to 8.00pm only)
Fax: 01684 560266
E-mail: margareteverton@onetel.com
Best in Show Winner - 2005

Understanding a show schedule and filling out forms

Show schedules are fairly self-explanatory but you must be very careful to enter all details clearly and accurately. You will be asked for your dog's name, its breed, sex, date of birth and the name of the breeder. In addition you will have to give full names of the sire and dam. You will then have to decide in which class or classes you would like to enter your dog.

On another page of the schedule (or on many different pages at the large shows) you will find a list of each breed that is classified at the show and also details of the variety classes. Each class will usually be given a number and it is this number that you must enter alongside the details given above.

Each show will offer different classifications, and at some shows there may not even be classes for your specific breed, in which case you may enter your dog in a variety class only. However, if there are breed classes suitable for your dog you are obliged to enter one of these as a priority (unless your dog is a puppy and there are no breed puppy classes on offer). This done, you may also enter in Variety classes if you wish.

The most usual breed classes you will find in your schedule are Minor Puppy, Puppy, Junior, Yearling, Maiden, Novice, Graduate, Post Graduate, Limit, Open and possibly Veteran, but there are several other classes available at some shows, though by no means all. The first four and the last (Veteran) are limited to exhibits of a certain age, details of which will be given in the show schedule. In each case the qualifying date is that of the first day of the show, not the day on which your breed is being judged, and you must bear in mind that some shows last over a period of three or four days.

In Britain the youngest age at which a dog can be entered for official competition is six months so, for instance, a Minor Puppy class is for dogs of six and not exceeding nine calendar months of age on the first day of the show; the Puppy class allows entry for dogs between six and twelve months.

This means that if you have a puppy that is eligible for the Minor Puppy class, you may if you wish enter it also in the Puppy Class, where it will be a 'seen dog'. Indeed you can also technically enter your young puppy in classes beyond that too, but I would urge caution here because your youngster will meet older competitors and his or her age will undoubtedly show.

Another point worth considering is that even if your puppy is only young, say seven months, it need not necessarily be entered in the Minor Puppy Class, but can go straight into Puppy. This can be a useful ploy if your puppy is rather large or mature for its age! It can also be useful if you have two puppies from the same litter; rather than have them compete against each other, one can go in Minor Puppy and the other in Puppy.

These Bernese Mountain Dogs have been securely tied around a tree in the shade, whilst awaiting their classes.

Junior and Yearling Classes

Dogs between the ages of six and eighteen months are eligible for entry in the Junior Class. For entry in a Yearling class they must be between twelve and twenty-four months. But don't let your enthusiasm as a new exhibitor take too much of a hold of you; – think twice before entering a raw six month old puppy in the Junior class for he will be up against strong competition from dogs who are much older both in mind and body! It is perfectly possible that a dog that has done a great deal of winning is entered in these classes, because the only restriction is age, not wins previously attained.

Veteran

Dogs entered in Veteran must be not less than seven years on the first day of the show and at a few shows there are also Special Veteran classes with a higher minimum age limit. Obviously if your dog is too old or infirm to enjoy showing it would be unfair to take him along, but many an 'oldie' is still in fine fettle at a ripe old age and thoroughly loves the occasional outing to a show. Often judges love judging these classes of older exhibits and the high form in which many dogs are shown almost defies belief.

Classes restricted according to wins

Entry in other classes is limited to the amount of winning your dog has done. The Open class is, as its name implies, open to all, including champions, but champions may not enter any of the other classes unless they are eligible by dint of their age.

Another highly competitive class is Limit. In this class, although champions are not eligible for entry, a dog may have won two Challenge Certificates or six first prizes in breed classes at Championship Shows in the Limit or Open classes.

It is from the Limit and Open classes that winning dogs or bitches can gain a coveted Kennel Club Stud Book Number (also gained from winning a Junior Warrant, Reserve CC or CC). This means that an entry is made in the KC Stud Book and that the dog will have qualified for Crufts for life. How many places, and whether it is just in the Open class or also in the Limit class that one can qualify for this recognition, depends upon the Kennel Club's classification of each breed in the Stud Book, this classification made primarily according to numerical strength.

In some breeds it is rather frowned upon to exhibit in these classes unless a dog has done considerable winning and has effectively 'won' its way through. However, if you feel your dog is worthy of entry in such high classes there is technically nothing to prevent you from entering, but you must bear in mind that your exhibit will come up against the very strongest competition, so there is far less chance of winning a prize card.

Times have certainly changed over recent decades. When I began showing dogs in the 1970s opinions were much stronger about not entering in these classes unless one's dog had won its way through, but now many people seem prepared to take the gamble. I notice this is something that many seasoned exhibitors and professional handlers do, because they know that a judge is more likely to award the CC or Reserve CC to winners from Limit and Open classes, though certainly not always.

At the outset of your dog's show career when he has done little if any winning, you may like to enter in the appropriate age class and perhaps Maiden or Novice. Maiden is

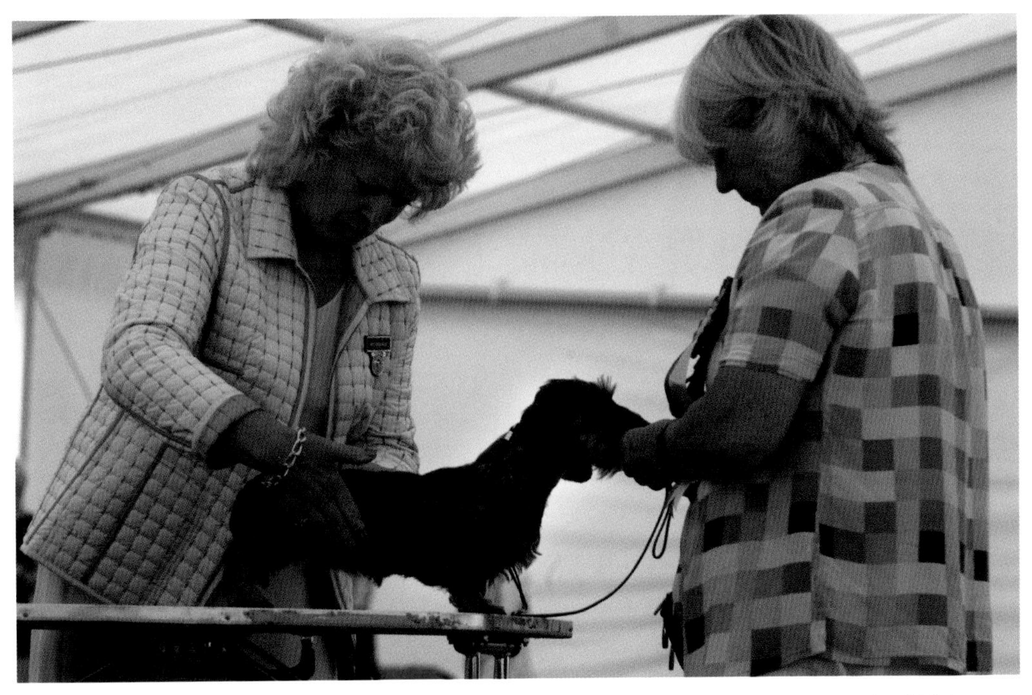

Judge assessing a Miniature Wirehaired Dachshund from the famous Drakesleat Kennel, which has produced over a hundred UK Champions.

for dogs that have not won a Challenge Certificate or a First Prize at an Open or Championship Show (Minor Puppy, Special Minor Puppy, Puppy and Special Puppy classes excepted, whether restricted or not). Novice is similar in all respects except that the dog may not have won three First Prizes as listed above.

As you are perhaps beginning to see, it is very necessary to read the small print on your show schedule if you are not going to make a mistake. If you arrive at a show having entered your dog in an incorrect class, if young it can be transferred to the correct age class, but if over qualified it can only be transferred to Open.

It would be impossible to present here all the permutations regarding which classes you may and may not enter, but you will hopefully see from the illustrations given above that you really must pay very careful attention to the schedule when making your show entries.

To complete your entry you will need to provide your name, address and telephone number, but if you wish you can prevent these being published in the show's catalogue by ticking the appropriate box. Carefully calculate the sum owed for the classes you have entered and, if you are offered the opportunity, you may choose to pre-pay for your catalogue which is likely to be a little more expensive purchased at the show, or may even not be available at all. Depending upon the size of the show you may also need to pre-pay for your car park and if you are a caravanning enthusiast, details of this may also be included on your form. When paying by cheque, be sure to put your name, address and

Every possible grooming accessory is available for purchase at major Championship Shows. (CUNLIFFE)

If you can't find exactly the right bedding you need for your dog in the local pet store, you are certain to find it at a dog show. (CUNLIFFE)

the name of your breed on the back of the cheque. Many larger societies now also offer a credit card payment facility.

As you will see, it can take quite a while to get used to entering your show schedules, so be sure to allow yourself plenty of time and post them off on or preferably before the closing date for entries.

To prevent any discrepancy about whether you did or did not enter the show, which can occasionally happen due to postal disputes or lost mail, it is always wise to obtain proof of postage from your post office, rather that just dropping the envelope in the box.

Obtaining the equipment you will need

The amount of equipment you will need will, to a large extent, be dependent upon your breed. Hopefully when you bought your puppy you will have been given good advice as to the most suitable grooming items needed for your particular dog. Hopefully, you will also have had a chance to read books about your breed and in some of these there will have been chapters about care, which may have shown photographs of the grooming procedure.

Every dog's coat is different, which is why such a wide range of combs, brushes, shampoos, conditioners and grooming sprays is available at shows. (CUNLIFFE)

Although most pet shops sell items such as combs, brushes and leads, you are unlikely to find the wide variety available at a dog show, nor are you likely to get such good advice from the sales person. If you can take yourself off to a general Championship Show, you will find numerous stalls selling all manner of equipment; indeed more than you ever dreamed possible. Most Open Shows and some Breed Shows also have such stalls, but there may be only one or perhaps two, so you won't have such a wide selection from which to choose. If yours is a trimmed breed and requires clippers, or perhaps a high-powered hairdryer especially for dogs, you will certainly need to purchase these at a show where you will be able to compare one item with another.

You may also need a grooming table and a trolley, not to mention a dog crate, so if this is the case a visit to a general championship show is a virtual 'must'.

As time goes on you will get to know which shampoos, conditioners and grooming sprays suit your dog's coat best, so always make sure you have plenty in stock, for if you have selected a specialist product that is sold at shows, there is a high risk that you won't be able to obtain it at a local pet shop. Some of the specialist dog grooming outlets now have web sites, so it is often possible to order by post if you have not worked out correctly quite how much shampoo you will have used before the next show!

These two exhibitors are wonderfully well equipped to enjoy their day at the show with their Toy breed.

Thinking about your outfit

Dog showing today has come on in leaps and bounds over the last few decades. Yes, a dog show is certainly a beauty show for dogs, but it is essential that exhibitors also dress to complement their exhibits. You have doubtless spent time, money and energy getting your dog into tip-top condition for the show, so surely you will not want to let him down by looking something of a mess yourself?

Of course no-one is suggesting that you change your own personal dress style to enter into the dog showing world, but as an exhibitor you should at least present yourself neatly. On the other hand, it is unwise to overdress for the occasion, after all it is your dog the judge will be assessing, not you, and the last thing you want to do is steal the limelight from your dog.

Initially there are the practicalities of your dress code to consider. Unless you are particularly comfortable walking quickly in high-heeled stiletto shoes on any surface, you would be best advised to wear something a little safer. Not only do you not want to step on your dog causing possible injury, but you do not want to trip over, or get your heel caught down some grating which might just happen to appear in the judging ring. The quality of ring surfaces varies enormously; they may be on carpet, concrete or some other hard surface, or on grass, which may not always be as short as you would wish and may or may not have the occasional pothole. If the show you are attending is in an equestrian centre, this will be yet another surface, compacted and more suited to horses than to humans in high heels!

In a leisure centre such as is frequently used for indoor dog shows, the society will most probably have provided rubber matting to give the dogs a firmer grip when they are moving, but the uncovered surfaces can sometimes be quite slippery, so beware!

As to clothing, this is also a matter for very careful consideration, and a lot will depend upon the size and especially the colour of dog you are showing. Most importantly you will not want a flowing skirt that is likely to blow across your dog's face obstructing his vision as he moves, nor will you want it to obstruct the judge's view of your exhibit.

Often a Scottish judge wears his kilt when judging at a prestigious show, as does Mr Donaldson when judging Cavaliers at Crufts.

If you are wearing a jacket with your outfit it should ideally be one that fits sufficiently comfortably that it can be buttoned up, at least when you are moving your dog. This again is to prevent anything flapping and causing obstruction, particularly if the bottom of your jacket is roughly level with the dog's head. And if in the summer your wardrobe includes plenty of low-cut blouses, please consider that you will be almost certain to have to bend over your dog at some point in the exhibition ring. Need I say more?

In actual fact, if you are comfortable wearing one, I always feel that a nicely tailored trouser suit is usually a good bet for ladies. For men, show attire is rather less hazardous, but I would suggest that the gentlemen amongst you steer clear of wearing hats in the ring on a windy day, for you will need to be concentrating on your dog, not on the whereabouts of your headgear.

Now to the tricky subject of your choice of colour of clothing. This will depend very much on the colour of your exhibit and if you happen to have two dogs to show, one black and one white, you will have to plan very carefully indeed.

Let us assume that you have a solid black dog. Whatever its size you will not want to dress entirely in black yourself, or the dog's outline will be completely lost. You may initially think, for example, that you could wear a light coloured skirt or trouser with a black jacket. Indeed that would look very smart, but whether or not it will work for you will depend on the size of your dog and whether or not you will bend down to show it. If yours is a small breed that is best displayed by you kneeling down low when the dog is standing for the judge's final assessment, your black jacket will end up just behind your dog, so again the outline will be lost.

Just supposing you have a particoloured dog that is a combination of black and white, you will probably select a nice bright colour, such as red, that will do justice to both and allow the complete outline to be seen. Wearing dark blue, for example, will enable the white parts to be seen clearly, but the black will get lost.

You will also have to consider that you will probably need to have a pocket available in which to keep your dog's titbits, and perhaps a comb. Some people who show breeds that are constantly baited often wear a special little bag around their waist to accommodate some fabulously smelly items without soiling their outfit.

Another special piece of equipment that you will need, this time for yourself, not for your dog, will be a ring-clip or an armband to display your ring number. Which you choose to wear is a matter of personal preference and both can be purchased at a show. Ring-clips can be simple or ornate, costing a few pence or several pounds

So, the cost of showing your dog might possibly have risen a little whilst you have been reading these last few paragraphs, but if you are lucky you will already have a suitable wardrobe to accommodate your dog's very special needs.

A convenient way of transporting your Welsh Corgi to and from the showground, without getting his feet and tummy soiled. (CUNLIFFE)

Working out your transport

Most dog exhibitors travel to shows by private car, but there are also coach services to most of the major shows or, depending on where you live, even the plane or ferry boat might be an option.

If travelling by car it is important that your car fits the purpose. That is to say that your dog or possibly dogs, which inevitably increase in number as you are bitten by the show-bug, can fit comfortably inside with all the equipment you will need for the day. Those who show small dogs can usually manage quite easily with a small hatch back or estate car, but larger breeds will very probably need a people carrier or 4 x 4. Owners of giant breeds, such as the Great Dane or Irish Wolfhound, often transport their dogs in vans which have been suitably fitted out with partitioning to suit their needs.

Some dogs simply refuse to jump up into the back of a fairly high vehicle, which can put a great strain on one's back as you hoist up a hefty canine into the back of your people carrier, not to mention the embarrassment of the entire performance! Should this present a problem, ramps are now available so that your dog, with care, can be trained to walk up the ramp and into the car.

Ventilation will also need to be carefully considered, for even on a relatively cool day heat can build up quickly inside a car and the consequences can be deadly. You must be able to easily access your dogs when travelling, just in case you are stuck in a traffic jam causing an unexpected build-up of heat because the car remains at a standstill.

Always carry with you a plentiful supply of fresh water, so that your dog can be offered a drink at any time, and in emergency the dog can be doused with

This Chinese Crested Dog of the Powder Puff variety and the Pug below are perfectly happy in their spanking new crate. (CUNLIFFE)

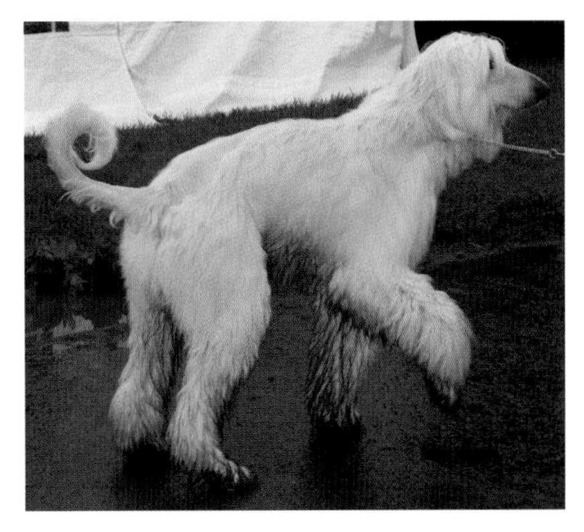

Allowing a freshly bathed Afghan Hound to get dirty is very disheartening.

water to avoid heatstroke. Depending on the arrangements in your vehicle, it will also most probably be useful to carry a 'space blanket' (which reflects the heat away when the silver side is uppermost) so that you can cover your dog's crate with this if there is danger of a build-up of heat. Never, ever leave your dog unattended in a car when you reach the show. Most shows now have people monitoring car parks for dogs that have been left in cars and if there is the slightest sign of distress your car number will be publicly tannoyed. If you do not return immediately there will be no hesitation about breaking into the car to save the distress of the dog.

When planning your car journey, always bear in mind that there may be a queue to get into the show at peak times when the majority of exhibitors are arriving. If you are heading for a dog show held in conjunction with an agricultural show, also be prepared to meet a lot of heavy vehicles travelling to the show with livestock, which will slow down the traffic still further. You may have been issued with a car park pass for the bigger shows, so have this to hand so that you can follow the sign for the right one, as there may be several.

If you don't already have a trolley, you will be able to purchase one at a show, and whilst at the stall you may even like to enquire about a specially designed dog bath.

As well as your car park pass, for major Championship Shows you will also have been sent a pass for your dog and a catalogue voucher if ordered. You will also need these at the very beginning of the day, so keep them easily to hand. In fact you will also need your dog's pass for release from the show, so when it has been checked, make sure you keep it in a safe place for when you leave the show.

This may sound a little pedantic, but also be sure you remember where you parked the car. In which car park and near which landmark? And don't use a handy high-sided vehicle as a landmark; it will probably have gone before you return to look for your own!

A perfect means of transport for a less-abled exhibitor with this well behaved Bichon Frisé.

If you need or choose to travel by coach, you will probably have found in your schedule details of people operating coaches especially to that show. Some are also advertised in the weekly canine press. Many people enjoy travelling this way, especially if they are making the journey alone, in which case it can indeed be more cost effective. However, by travelling this way you have far less flexibility of course. You will have to meet the coach at a predestined pick-up point and the coach will be scheduled to leave at a certain time, usually prior to the close of the show. If you are fortunate enough to have won Best of Breed with your dog and therefore have to compete in Group Judging or for Best in Show, arrangements will usually be made for the coach to depart later, but inevitably this can play havoc with the collection plans of other exhibitors who were expecting to reach their destination earlier.

If you are travelling from mainland Britain to a show in Ireland, or the other way around, you will need to transport your dog by ferry or by plane. In the latter case you must be very careful to check that the air booking has been made correctly to avoid disappointment upon arrival at the airport. Some airlines take only a very limited number of dogs, and some do not take dogs at all.

When travelling by ferry, if you have arrived at the ferry by car and are taking it across too, your dog will remain in the car during the crossing, so make sure he has every comfort available to him and access to plenty of water. Kennels are usually available as an alternative, but your dog would probably be much happier in the familiar environment of your car.

Now that Britain has less stringent quarantine laws, it is possible for people from some foreign countries to exhibit their dogs in Britain, and vice versa. However, a strict health programme with certification is imperative under the 'Pets Passport' scheme, so such a trip will have to be planned well in advance so that any necessary vaccinations and health records are in place in good time.

Things to Think About

How do I locate a good ringcraft class?

Where do I find out about forthcoming shows?

I must be careful when completing my entry forms.

I shall need to keep careful records too.

Where can I buy the equipment I need?

What shall I wear to show my dog?

Planning my transport to the show.

I need to remember water and ventilation.

CHAPTER 3

WHAT KIND OF SHOW?

The dog showing world is much larger than you might imagine, with various different levels of show, some for all breeds, some for breeds within one Group and some breed specific. Most shows are licensed by the Kennel Club (KC), but there are others that are not, such as Terrier Shows, these often being held at Game Shows and attracting quite a different group of participants to those in the show world of KC registered pedigree breeds.

The Kennel Club frowns heavily on anyone participating in a show that is not KC licensed, but it has to be said that there are some breeds, such as the Lucas Terrier, that have elected not to have their breed registered with the KC because in doing so they feel they would lose their autonomy which, in their opinion, helps the breed to forge ahead and survive. The Lucas Terrier fraternity keeps very careful records concerning breeding programmes and the breeders' hearts are very much in the right place, as is the case with several other breeds that elect not to fall under the auspices of the KC.

Other countries have different Kennel Clubs that operate under different rules. In many countries the Federation Cynoligique Internationale is the governing body, whilst in America it is the American Kennel Club and in Southern Ireland the Irish Kennel Club. These three are recognised by the Kennel Club, but there are others that are not. Understandably different breeds of dog are shown in different countries, and by no means all breeds that exist on this globe are to be found in the UK.

These Airedale Terrier enthusiasts have raised the fantastic sum of over £2,000.00 for Cancer Research.

Because of the international nature of our hobby, and in particular with the quarantine laws being lessened in the UK, often dogs travel from one country or even continent to another to be shown. Likewise many of the very experienced judges find themselves officiating in countries other than their own, always an exciting and interesting experience for a judge. This also provides exhibitors with an opinion from a judge who probably views the breed from a different perspective.

There are so very many types of show worldwide that it would be virtually impossible to describe them all in detail, so the following is intended to guide you through the KC registered shows that are open to exhibitors in Britain. With the exception of Crufts (where the minimum age is eight months unless a younger puppy has already gained entry into the Stud Book), at all shows in Britain the minimum age for competition is six months, though at some Breed Shows, puppies from the age of four months may be taken along to the show, but not entered for competition.

Companion Dog Shows

The most casual type of show is the Companion Dog Show, organised under KC rules, but raising funds for a charity or charitable cause. Dogs are taken along on the day to participate in the show, so there is no form filling several weeks prior to the show day. This means that an exhibitor might just awake one sunny weekend morning and decide to take his dog along for an enjoyable day out.

There are usually classes for both pedigree and non-pedigree dogs, and even the pedigree exhibits need not necessarily be registered with the KC. There are usually various Any Variety Pedigree classes, such as Any Variety Sporting, Any Variety Non-Sporting, Any Variety Puppy (six to twelve months) and so on. In addition there are what are known as Novelty or 'Fun' classes and these are open to all dogs, so if you have a pedigree dog and a mongrel, they can both go along and enjoy the outing.

The relaxed atmosphere of a Companion Dog Show.

This Boxer's colouring would not allow him to enter one of the major shows, but he is patiently awaiting his class at a Companion Show.

The Novelty classes can include 'Best Condition', 'Best Expression', 'Waggiest Tail', 'Dog That Looks Most Like Owner', 'Dog the Judge Would Like to Take Home'; the options are endless. There can even be fancy dress classes and frequently the owners kit themselves out in fancy dress, as well as the dogs!

Entry fees are cheap and it's good to know that what you are spending on your day of fun is going to a good cause. Because of the very nature of these shows, there are often prizes on offer for class winners, even down to fourth or fifth place. These prizes will usually have been sponsored, in an endeavour to swell the entries and increase the funds for whatever charitable cause has been selected.

Such shows usually stand alone, but they can sometimes be held in conjunction with a larger show. Besides classes to assess dogs' beauty points there may also be classes to test a dog's skill in obedience. However, tests for Obedience at Companion Shows are different from those laid down in the KC's Rules and Regulations at other shows. Agility Tests can also be held, but again these differ from the norm. Another event that is becoming increasing popular at Companion Dog Shows is Heelwork to Music, not on a competitive basis, but as a demonstration.

In the pedigree classes at these shows there are rules that prevent dogs that have done any substantial amount of winning from entering; Challenge Certificate, Reserve Challenge Certificate and Junior Warrant winners cannot compete. This technically means that for the novice dog and exhibitor, there is more chance of winning a prize. However, the standard of judging at a Companion Show is indeed varied. Some very notable and highly experienced judges often take the centre of the ring to officiate for a good cause, but just as frequently the judges have rather limited experience and may never even have judged some of the breeds that are exhibited. Many of the shows, though, have two judges, one for the pedigree classes and one, perhaps a local personality, for the Novelty ones. This means you will at least be able to obtain the opinion of two judges on the same day and the chances are that you and your dogs will have had a jolly good day out.

Matches

Matches are a form of competition where judging is by elimination, one dog against another. They may be held between dogs that belong to one society, such as a ringcraft club, or can be when dogs from one club compete against those from another. Clubs may hold up to twelve Matches each year and so quite a lot of ringcraft clubs hold one each month. This provides a little competition in a friendly atmosphere, and makes a change from the weekly routine, thereby providing dogs with a slightly different chance to practise and to show off their skills.

For a dog to be entered in a Match, the owner must be a member of the society that is hosting the Match, or of the invited club. All dogs entered must be registered with the KC, and no dog that has won a Challenge Certificate or any award counting toward the title of Champion under KC rules is eligible for competition.

Matches are a good training ground for the novice dog and exhibitor, for they are very much smaller than shows, there being a maximum of sixty-four dogs eligible to compete. Most such events are held in the evenings, and there may even be a short ringcraft session prior to the commencement of the Match, so there is absolutely no reason why you should not go along to your ringcraft class as usual, and in many cases you will have the chance to decide on the night whether or not you wish to join in. If the club is holding a Match against another society, that is a slightly different matter as the organisers will need to be sure of numbers beforehand so participants may be fixed a week or so in advance.

Limited Shows

Limited Shows are no longer held frequently in the UK, but they do exist and provide a good initial training ground in a fairly relaxed atmosphere without too much stress. There can be no more than seventy-five classes at any Limited Show and the restrictions as to which dogs may compete is the same as for a Match. Exhibitors must be members of the society holding the show, but this is a simple procedure and can usually be done at the time of entry, by completing an extra section on the entry form.

Because some class definitions vary at a Limited Show from those at Open and Championship Shows, it is, as always, important to read the class definitions very carefully before making your entry. Sometimes Limited Shows are so small that they are held in the evening in somewhere like a village hall, and often only one judge officiates for the entire show. Usually refreshments are available, and once again such shows provide an ideal 'first step' for the newer exhibitor.

Although some Limited Shows are open to all breeds, usually with plenty of Any Variety classes from which to choose, others are breed specific shows, limited to just one breed. In all cases the judges at these shows are selected by the host society.

Open Shows

There used to be a time when every new showgoer began to learn the ropes at Limited and Open Shows, but sadly that attitude is increasingly becoming a thing of the past and everyone seems to want to rush into the showring at Championship level. This, I feel, is a great pity, for Open Shows have a great deal to offer, especially for the newer exhibitor, although many seasoned showgoers enjoy them too.

This lovely Pug won a place in the Toy Group in Scotland.

People rarely travel enormous distances to All-Breed Open Shows, so they frequently provide an ideal opportunity to meet other breed enthusiasts who live within fifty miles or so of your own home. Through exhibiting at these shows many a friendship builds up whilst sitting around the ringside waiting for your own breed to be shown. Few Open Shows have benching for the dogs, so the atmosphere is relatively informal, with people and dogs mingling together.

Open Shows can be large or small, often dependent upon the geography of the venue. Sometimes they even span a two day period, some Groups being judged on the first day and others on the second, with the first day's overall adult and puppy winners returning the next day to compete for Best in Show and Best Puppy in Show.

The general format is that a few Variety classes, such as for Puppies, are held at the beginning of the day, then the individual breeds that are classified follow on and toward the close of the day are more Variety and Stakes classes. The number of rings varies according to the size of the show, but there are usually four or more. Again the venue and the time of year will be the deciding factor as to whether judging is indoors or out, but frequently if judging is held in a leisure centre some breeds are inside, whilst the larger breeds, such as German Shepherd Dogs that need plenty of space while they are being gaited, have their own rings outside.

As with Matches and the shows already mentioned above, it is the hosting society that selects the judges, but if there are four or more classes scheduled for a breed (six for a few numerically strong breeds classified on the 'E' list according to the Kennel Club Stud Book) the judge concerned must be on a breed club's 'B' list, denoting that he or she already has some experience of judging that particular breed. The amount of experience necessary varies from breed to breed, and indeed from club to club, largely in view of the numerical strength of the breed in question.

Judges who officiate at an Open Show for Variety classes, must already be Championship Show judges of at least one breed, which means that they already have several years of experience and have been approved by the KC to judge at this level. These same judges will also usually be found judging some individual breeds at an Open Show, so as an exhibitor you can rest assured that such judges already have considerable experience, although not necessarily in that particular breed.

All the activity of an Open Show, with dogs being groomed near the side of the ringside. (CUNLIFFE)

But an Open Show is also a training ground for new judges, and can indeed provide a very first judging appointment, however until you have had some experience as an exhibitor you will not be in a position to know which judges are more experienced in your breed than others when you complete your entry form. Nonetheless, win or lose, exhibition at Open Shows provides a very good training ground, both for you and your dog. Also, if you are fortunate enough to win some classes and the numbers present in that class are sufficient, you will have the opportunity to clock up points which will count towards a Junior Warrant (JW) or a Show Certificate of Merit (Sh CM).

Although most Open Shows do not provide the opportunity to qualify for Crufts, at what are called Premier Open Shows a very few dogs do qualify and this will be clearly stated on the show schedule. Quite often, winners of the major awards at these shows become eligible to compete in an annual award for 'Top Dog', usually held as a Special Event in a local geographical area, so there are lots of good things to look forward to if your dog wins well at Open level.

Apart from All-Breed Open Shows, most breed clubs also hold one Open Show a year and the judge at this is normally someone who has considerable experience of judging the breed, but does not yet award Challenge Certificates. Judging such a show is usually an important rung on the ladder if they are eventually to judge at Championship level.

At most of these shows a very pleasant atmosphere prevails. The size of the show and number of entries will inevitably vary according to the breed. In some cases there are even two judges, one for dogs and one for bitches. In this case a referee has to be appointed, to make any final decisions on major winners if the two judges fail to agree as to which is the best, as often happens!

Sometimes varieties of a breed hold joint Open Shows, so that, for example, Miniature Schnauzers, Schnauzers and Giant Schnauzers are all judged at the same venue on the same day, usually with different judges for each variety and one judge elected to award Best in Show.

Championship Shows

At the very top end of the scale are Championship Shows, although as I have already mentioned, some new exhibitors are tempted to plunge in headlong and actually begin their hobby of showing at Championship Shows. Such competition is a costly business, so frankly, unless you know your dog is good enough for such high level competition, I really think you would be well-advised to begin at a lower level, which is just as much fun and far less stressful.

It is at Championship Shows that dogs compete for the coveted title of Champion, or Show Champion in those breed, such as Gundogs and Border Collies, that also require success in the field to hold the full title of Champion. But only a few dogs reach such dizzy heights. It is indeed not unknown for an exhibitor to make her very first dog up to the title of Champion, but other people show for years and years, still without reaching this particular goal.

This Golden Retriever won 4th in the Puppy Group at a Championship Show specifically for Gundogs.

At some Championship Shows all breeds that have separate breed classification are eligible for Challenge Certificates, but at many some breeds are separately classified, although without Challenge Certificates on offer. A win in such a class counts for no more than a win in a breed class at an Open Show but still the Best of Breed winner is allowed to compete in the Group ring and, if it is fortunate enough to win that, for Best in Show.

Championship Shows have quite a different atmosphere from the smaller shows and events. To begin with they are usually spread over a three or four day period, the winners of each of the seven Group competitions returning on the last day to compete for Best in Show. Sometimes there are also Puppy Groups and competition for Best Puppy in Show, but by no means always.

Show grounds are often vast, with large car parks, tents in which dogs are benched,

Gundogs being judged in a splendid indoor ring at Driffield Championship Dog Show.

covered areas used as judging rings if the weather is inclement, loads of rings outside, usually on the grass, and many, many stalls selling all manner of doggy items, as well as refreshments for those of us of the human variety.

Competition is hot, very hot! There is rarely any prize money on offer, except perhaps for the top winners, but it is the prestige of winning at such a show that counts. Once again points can be earned toward Junior Warrants. And of course there may be the chance of winning a Challenge Certificate (CC), three of which, if awarded by different judges give a dog the title of Champion, provided that one is awarded after the dog is one year old. When CCs are on offer, in most cases the judge may award one to the Best of each sex, though he is at liberty to withhold the CC, should he not think any of the dogs is worthy of the award. Three CCs does not sound many, but Britain is the hardest place in the world to make up a Champion because a dog has to compete against other dogs that already hold the title. This makes it exceedingly difficult.

The judge may also award a Reserve Challenge Certificate (RCC), which states that he considers this dog, too, to be worthy of the title of champion. Should the CC winner be disqualified for some reason the CC is awarded to the RCC winner in lieu; otherwise this award does not count toward the title of Champion – but it is very pleasing to win one as it proves how highly the judge has thought of one's dog.

There are other classes at Championship Shows too; sometimes Variety classes for breeds that do not have separate classification, Stakes classes, in which there is prize money on offer, and classes for Rare Breeds and those still on the Import Register. So, whatever breed of dog you have selected as your first show dog, you are almost certain to find an opportunity to show it at a Championship Show.

But don't think you will necessarily go home emblazoned with rosettes if you have won at such a show. Usually the only rosettes on offer are for the dogs to which a judge has awarded Best of Sex or Best Puppy, to the Stakes winners and to those that have won Group placings, or of course Best in Show.

Apart from All-Breed Championship Shows, there are some Championship Shows just for one Group of dogs, or two in the case of the Working and Pastoral Groups. Other Championship Shows are breed club events and it is generally considered a very high honour for a judge to be selected to judge at one of these. Frequently at Breed Shows there are rather more dogs present than at an all-breeds show. Exhibitors do not have to be members of the club but many of them are, and although the show has all the tension of a Championship event, there is generally a very pleasant atmosphere as so many people know each other. The entry fee is almost always less than at an All-Breed Championship Show, in part because there is rarely any benching for the dogs, which keeps down the cost.

There are usually a few stalls at Breed Shows, some to help raise funds for the club whilst providing a service to members, and there is almost certainly a raffle or tombola, another means of raising funds, which are sometimes given to a charity such as the breed's rescue section. At a Breed Club Championship Show it is all hands to the deck to get things organised, and a lot of hard work goes into putting on the event. This is handled by Officers and Committee of the club, possibly with a few additional helpers. Depending on the venue that is being used, catering may be provided by the owners of the venue or by the committee. In the latter case, prices are usually very reasonable and it is always good if exhibitors can support 'the kitchen' as once again this is an important aspect of helping to raise funds for the club.

Most exhibitors are prepared to travel many miles to exhibit at a Championship Show, so the cost can certainly mount up, but it is only at this type of show that dogs can gain a championship title and, after all, I suppose that's what we all aspire to.

The Young Kennel Club

The Young Kennel Club (YKC) is for young dog lovers aged between six and twenty-four. Its purpose is to encourage interest in care, training and other activities associated with dogs. Apart from education in the care and training of dogs, it aims to develop courtesy, sportsmanship and self-discipline and, not least, to encourage a sense of responsibility toward dog ownership.

Through the YKC, young people are able to participate in all activities connected with dogs and can help with their management. In doing so they have plenty of opportunity to meet new friends, both human and canine, and have plenty of opportunity to learn many things about dogs.

Membership of the YKC is currently £10 per year for which members receive a membership certificate, a badge, four newsletters a year and a membership pack customised to their age range and containing a free gift. Each membership pack contains a beginners' guide to handling, agility, obedience, flyball, stakes and heelwork to music. Armed with this essential information every young newcomer to the world of dogs will find some aspect to enjoy.

This young lady already presents her Italian Greyhound to perfection, her family having chosen a breed of a size that is highly suitable for a young exhibitor.

Young Kennel Club Utility Winner with a Standard Poodle.

A happy line up of Young Kennel Club winners and their dogs.

Apart from the KC's own events, put on especially for its young members, various dog clubs hold YKC classes throughout the year, giving them an opportunity to qualify for Crufts. Indeed the YKC provides opportunities to train and, for the more experienced, to compete.

Another feature of the YKC is YKC Awards. By attending classes, its members can gain certificates and badges for various different things. Each year the YKC also holds a National Training Camp for members between the ages of eight and sixteen. Organised by Senior Members, the week is packed full of training and social activities, offering a great opportunity to socialise and have fun with dogs.

The Senior Members, whose ages range from sixteen to twenty-four, get the chance to attend an Outward Bound Development Course each year. This focuses on teamwork, confidence, sportsmanship and communication skills, as well problem solving, leadership and project management, thereby enabling these young people to apply their skills when helping with the organisation of the YKC.

The YKC at Crufts and other major shows

At Crufts there is a complete ring dedicated to YKC participants, with a full programme of activities each day. A daily schedule might comprise Starters Obedience, Agility Dog of the Year, Elementary Obedience, Heelwork to Music, an Obedience Presentation, Show Handling, Stakes classes and even a Biathlon, combining agility with obedience. To take part in these events members have to have qualified, the actual qualification varying depending upon the event.

At other shows there are also plenty of different classes on offer in which YKC members can compete. Typically there may be YKC Members Stakes classes, YKC Handling classes divided into the various different age groups.

Of course there is nothing to prevent YKC members entering in normal breed classes, and many of them do. Indeed even the occasional exhibitor who is too young to become a member of the YKC enters a breed class, and with a good dog, well presented and shown, they sometimes win high awards!

This talented young handler is not competing in YKC classes but in the main Group ring where she has won Best of Breed with a Soft Coated Wheaten Terrier. Already she is showing signs of handling dogs with the same expertise as her highly successful mother.

Crufts

Crufts is considered the most highly prestigious show in the world and now attracts an entry of over 22,000 exhibits, spread over a period of four days. Earlier it was held at London's Olympia, then at Earls' Court and moved to the National Exhibition Centre near Birmingham in 1991 when it celebrated its Centenary Show, attracting a record entry of 22,993 dogs. Here the show can have all the space it needs, so that now there are six different halls, covering an area of 85,000 square metres. In these halls are many individual rings of substantial size and two main rings, one of which, with its famous green carpet, is the show place for each day's major winners when they compete for the main prizes. The culmination is Best in Show judging on the final night.

Leading up to and throughout the show, Crufts has good television coverage by the BBC and press reporters come along in their hundreds, from all over the world. The stalls and trade stands at the show need to be seen to be believed as there are over four hundred of them, so visitors can buy virtually everything they might need for their dogs – and more! Crufts is also a good place for the many canine charities to publicise their work, and in the main rings at Crufts there are frequent displays by Hearing Dogs for the Deaf, Search and Rescue organisations and Police Dog teams to name but a few. There are also demonstrations of the Good Citizen Dog Scheme, the largest dog training programme in the UK and there are many other exciting competitions such as Flyball and Agility so that, in all, over 6,000 dogs take part in displays and demonstrations.

Bearing in mind that there are roughly 14,000 dog exhibitors and over 120,000 public visitors to the show, Crufts is a veritable of hub of activity. There is also a Charitable Trust Auction, run by the KC, and a very popular attraction at the show is Discover Dogs, where all breeds recognised by the KC are on display, a few of which are not yet eligible for competition in this country.

Qualifying For Crufts

Because you are interested in showing your dog, your aim will be to qualify for Crufts each year, something that is easier to do in some breeds than in others. The KC confirms and publicises qualifications for entry each year, and because there might be variations from year to year it is necessary to check the exact requirements at the time.

If you are based in Britain and are qualifying your dog here, this is usually done by winning first, second or third place in a qualifying class at a Championship Show where CCs are on offer, but these classes are not the same for every breed, largely dependent upon its Stud Book Band. So numerically strong breeds like Whippets, Golden Retrievers, Boxers and Cavalier King Charles Spaniels have more classes in which to qualify, but then they have more competition. On the other hand, if you have a breed that has only a few exhibits being shown at each Championship show it is much more likely that you will qualify your dog for there may indeed be only three exhibits in your class. This means that although many of the dogs exhibited at Crufts are truly high quality specimens, others do sometimes get through the net, so you should never take it as read that every dog you see at that prestigious show is of the very highest quality.

Other dogs that are qualified for Crufts by right of their wins are Champions, Show Champions, Working Trials Champions and Obedience or Agility Champions under the rules of the KC. Equally if a dog has been awarded a Stud Book Number, or qualifies for entry in the KC Stud Book through Field or Working Trials it is eligible for Crufts entry. Once again, Stud Book qualification varies according to the breed, but if a dog has been awarded a Challenge Certificate or Reserve Challenge Certificate, a Stud Book Number is issued, whatever the breed.

So as you can see, entry for Crufts is quite a complicated affair. Also, if you are fortunate enough to qualify your dog, you must keep a careful record of where you won, on which date and as a result of which placing in your breed. This information will be needed when you complete your show entry form which, by the way, will have to be submitted well before the show, so keep a careful eye on the closing date.

Now that exhibitors from other countries can come to the UK with their dogs, in recent years the KC has set down rules for Crufts qualification for overseas exhibits too. Any Champion from a country with which the KC has a reciprocal agreement qualifies automatically if it is domiciled in the UK and is on the KC Breed Register, as do all FCI International Champions. Beyond this the rules laid down are highly complex, some shows being nominated on an annual basis enabling winners of certain classes at these shows to compete at Crufts. Although most of the European Community countries hold shows under the FCI system, bringing into play the FCI International Champion qualification, other countries do not. For this reason the KC has made special qualifying rules for the USA, Canada, Australia, Japan and New Zealand.

More and more overseas exhibitors come to Crufts each year, and many of their dogs win high accolades, making this truly the biggest and most renowned dog show in the entire world.

Other Major Championship Shows

Crufts is of course not the only important show of the year, and it has to be said that many exhibitors enjoy the more down-to-earth atmosphere of other big Championship Shows in preference to Crufts. Many of us prefer not to have to battle our way through the crowds of visitors and trade stands that we consider have little to do with dogs, and to get down to the real business of showing and mixing with like-minded folk. Nothing can detract from the splendour, spectacle and prestige of Crufts but so many other big shows are worthy of recognition.

Some exhibitors travel up and down the country to visit virtually every Championship Show, but for others this is of course simply not something they can consider, due to geography, time and expense.

One famous Deerhound lady, the late Miss Anastasia Noble (Ardkinglas), lived on Scotland's west coast but did not drive, so for her very long career in dogs she always travelled to shows by train and by taxi. I recall her telling me of one occasion when she had fallen asleep on the train and missed her station. Not so her dogs; they got off at the appointed stop and just sat there waiting for her arrival on the platform when she finally returned, having awoken at a later station and found her dogs missing!

Indeed dog exhibitors who live in the highlands of Scotland or at the tip of Cornwall, find it difficult to attend as many shows as others of us do. The Scottish Kennel Club shows, held twice each year at the Royal Highland Showground, Ingliston, near Edinburgh's airport, are understandably highly popular with the Scottish fraternity, but the show is attended by many other exhibitors too. Frequently it is the choice of judge that determines how far an exhibitor will travel. Experienced exhibitors know which judges are likely to appreciate their stock and which are not, so a long trip can be very worthwhile to exhibit under the 'right' judge. Conversely it is really not worth the long haul from Bournemouth to Scotland if the exhibitor entered under that year's judge on a previous occasion when his dogs were not even considered his dogs for the placings.

The Welsh Kennel Club show is in the stunning setting of the Welsh hills on the Royal Welsh Showground and is a very popular show for caravanners. The journey by road to the show is not the easiest, but the warm welcome one receives is well worth the trip. This show, like several others including those held at Three Counties Showground, is held at an agricultural venue. In fine weather the majority of judging is held outdoors, but if it is raining judging takes place in tented areas and in covered areas that most of us still call the 'cow sheds' – which are of course thoroughly cleaned out prior to the show! Such venues also have some large halls which can be used for certain breeds, and for the Best in Show ring, so that one can be certain that the odd hovering rain-cloud will not spoil the important Group judging at the end of each day and the Best in Show judging at the close of the show.

In Northern Ireland shows are held under the auspices of the Kennel Club (as opposed to Southern Ireland which works on a different system) and there is a Championship Show at Belfast each year, many exhibitors travelling over, usually by ferry, to campaign their dogs. A show popular with exhibitors from Cornwall and Devon is the Paignton show which uses a venue just at the end of the M5 motorway, making it accessible from all parts of the country, despite it being rather a long hike for some. Not all shows are held in the town of their name. The Manchester show outgrew its venue in central Manchester a few years ago and moved to the Bingley Hall near Stafford, a venue that plays host to many dogs shows, both Championship and Open alike. Indeed many of the major shows are held in the Midlands region and in general these do tend to draw particularly large entries for they are more easily accessible for a greater number of people.

Two Midland based shows with a wealth of historial background to them are the Birmingham National show and Ladies' Kennel Association, the latter being the very last all-breed Championship Show of the year, so a fitting place for exhibitors to exchange Christmas cards, gifts and greetings before the onset of the new year ahead.

Different Championship Shows tend to be known for different things. Windsor always springs to mind as a show that attracts a good many overseas visitors, whilst Richmond always reminds me of Junior Handlers and the YKC, for that's the show at which the Finals are held each year. Then there's the Hound Show, a major Championship Show just for dogs in the Hound Group, but here packs of working hounds also come along to take part in their own section of the show, and many visitors are interested to see them all together parading with the colourfully clad huntsmen.

A Rhodesian Ridgeback being shown in the main ring.

I am sure many people have their own favourite shows and it would be quite unfair to single out any one in particular, because each in its own way has something very special about it. The problem with travelling to shows is that all one's friends think dog-showing people travel up and down the country so much that they visit loads of different places. Actually that is far from the truth for it is rare that shows are held in the centre of a city, although Windsor is an obvious exception with splendid views of the Castle only a stone's throw away. Usually one loads the car before dawn, drives straight to and from the venue, returning home as darkness approaches, or in winter months long after it has fallen.

The Blackpool Show has now purchased its own land so is held a little distance away from the coast, but when it used to be nearer to the sea I always made myself drive along the promenade before wending my way home. It was fun to see the 'Kiss-me-Quick' hats and the candyfloss crammed into people's mouths. I rarely even got out of the car, but at least I travelled home with the distinct feeling that I'd been to the seaside!

Regular exhibitors get to know the various different big Championship Shows and where they are located, but from time to time venues change, due to the necessity to find a more suitable venue, or perhaps dates have clashed making the normal venue unavailable. A few years ago Southern Counties moved well away from its usual venue near Gatwick Airport to Thatcham, and Richmond has also made a change of venue recently, as has the South Wales Kennel Association and now Driffield too. But soon enough we all get used to the new route and the new setting, so that within a couple of years our cars will almost head straight for them without any need for a route planner!

Other Exhibitors and Handlers

Dog shows are great levellers. Here it is the dogs that count and it is not at all unusual for members of the nobility to rub shoulders with people with whom they would be unlikely to mix at another social level. Dog showing is quite an expensive sport, but there are many who scrimp and save to look after their dogs and to enter a few shows; others are more than comfortably off, but dogs bring them all together and if they are truly dedicated dog people, each realises that they have lots to learn from each other.

In dogs we never stop learning, but some people open themselves up to learning procedure better than others. I find it sad when exhibitors, particularly the newer ones, leave the show as soon as their own dog's class has finished. They could learn so much more if they stopped to watch completion of judging, at least in their own breed. They may not agree with the judge's placings, but only by watching can they learn to 'get their eye in' as we say. Also, around the ringside will be several exhibitors with a real depth of knowledge about their breed, sometimes in several breeds, and if you can get into conversation with them you will effectively be having a private lesson.

Many experienced showgoers are only too willing to give help and encouragement to newcomers. They will not want to get into deep conversation just before they are about to enter the ring, nor when they are grooming their dogs, but there is a usually a 'right time' for a chat and they will most probably welcome your enthusiasm.

Even when you are sitting alone by the ringside you can learn a great deal from the way other exhibitors show their dogs. Some of the handlers you watch will be true experts, indeed they may be professional handlers who take other people's dogs into the exhibition ring and charge a sum for doing so. Usually if they win highly at a show the dog's owner will have to pay a higher fee, so it is in the handler's interest to present these dogs to perfection.

Watch them carefully, see what they do, how they present and stand their dogs, how they move them at just the right speed, always keeping one eye on the dog and the other on the judge.

When you are in the ring with your dog, particularly at Championship Shows, you are almost certain to come up against other dogs that are probably better then your own, some of them handled by experts. Don't be too despondent if you don't beat them, for the chances are that if they are so proficient, either as breeders or handlers, they will only take good stock into the ring.

Many people relatively new to the world of dog shows make comments about it being the 'faces' that win, not the dogs. To some extent this can occasionally be true, but always remember that those with plenty of experience in the dog world know the quality of the stock they are taking into the ring. Yes, they may be better able to conceal the odd minor fault than you are at this stage, but they are unlikely to show a really bad dog, so many of them probably do deserve to win. But there is always another judge and another day, and the dogs you are competing against will be different at every show. In short, never get bitter about your losses, but in those early stages in your showing career, always keep your wits about you and learn as much as you possibly can from those more experienced than yourself.

Things to Think About

What type of dog shows are available to me?

Should I start at Championship or Open Shows?

How shall I display my rosettes?

Can I or a member of my family join the YKC?

How will I qualify my dog for Crufts?

What can I learn from others?

I must always remember to be polite, even if I lose.

CHAPTER 4

PREPARING YOUR DOG BEFORE THE SHOW

You will by now have recognised that there is a tremendous variety of dog breeds in the showring, each of them requiring particular presentation, some very much more than others. In addition, if you have been to a show as an onlooker, you will doubtless have observed that some people present their dogs very much better than others and usually it is the better presented dogs that win top honours. After all a dog show is a beauty contest. Of course a dog must be constructed correctly and be typical of its breed, but think of a beautifully constructed female model on the cat-walk – she wouldn't look quite the same if her hair was dirty and a mess, and she was wearing clothes that looked like a bag of rubbish, would she?

At your ringcraft classes you will hopefully have learned a lot about moving your dog in the ring and standing or stacking it for the judge's assessment. If you have access to a mirror so that you can see exactly the picture that you and your dog are making together, you will be in a better position to be self critical. It is all too easy to be 'kennel-blind', not recognising the faults your dog has. You will stand a much greater chance of success if you recognise your dog's faults as well as its virtues so that you can minimise the effects of the former and bring the latter to the fore.

Don't just practise moving your dog at ringcraft classes though. Make sure you take your dog out to public places so that it gets used to the various sounds it is likely to encounter at a show. Some breeds would hardly bolt if a bomb exploded near them, but others most certainly would, in addition to which even within a breed temperaments vary.

Lhasa Apsos are not always the easiest breed to show for their breed standard requires them to be 'aloof with strangers'. In their Tibetan homeland they would clearly not have come across the sort of sounds they are likely to encounter at a dog show where there can be all sorts of clutter made by people erecting dog crates near the ringside, dropping them accidentally and even the wind occasionally blowing the award boards down on a particularly blustery day. Many breeders I know make a habit of being noisy around the house when raising puppies, to accustom them to sudden loud sounds. Banging together saucepan lids seems to be a favourite, and although I personally refrain from that, I do like to be sure they have all heard the vacuum cleaner at close proximity.

I recall one prominent lady in this breed told me that she used to take each of her dogs to the local traffic island and stand in the middle of it for a while, obviously being absolutely certain that their collars and leads were utterly secure before doing so! (Just a word of warning, never use a show lead where your dog might run into danger if it slips its lead.)

Lhasa Apsos being one of my own breeds, I used a different method when preparing dogs for the ring. I used to take my dogs individually to the local shopping mall after the stores had closed, giving me the opportunity to walk them on different surfaces, even over grids and such like, for these can sometimes be found in indoor rings. They could hear all sorts of echoing sounds and maybe even young teenagers playing a noisy game. Just outside the mall was an open air market and the empty wooden tables made an excellent surface on which to practise stacking my dog for the invisible judge.

Empty car parks are also great places to practise moving dogs for the showring. If you have a large breed, here you are almost certain to find as much space as you need to allow your dog to practise gaiting at its very best speed. Obviously you will use your common sense as to when and where exactly to practise in this way!

Coat presentation

Clearly the long coated breeds require more work in presenting the coat to perfection, but never underestimate the devotion you will need to give to any dog to get it looking its best. Certainly never underestimate the demands made on those who show the Terrier breeds, many of which need expert stripping and trimming to give them the pucker jackets that make them look so spick and span in the ring.

To get any coat into good condition you will not only have to think about the coat from the outside, but from the inside too. Correct diet will not only play an important part in the general health of your dog, but also in the quality of its coat. This must never be overlooked, and if your dog's coat is perhaps lacking a little lustre or condition you should seriously consider changing the diet or adding supplements. Again I would urge you to ask around at the many stalls at major dog shows and take advice as to what might improve the situation. It might just be necessary to add a little cod-liver oil to the diet (bearing in mind that this can overheat the blood if used without discretion), or oil of evening primrose is excellent, although rather more expensive.

Lots of coat preparation is needed to get a Terrier in good show coat and looking like this Best of Breed winning West Highland White Terrier.

Smooth coats

The easiest coats to deal with are, understandably, those of the short and smooth coated breeds. Apart from a regular check of the obvious items such as nails, pads, ears and eyes, as is necessary in any breed, a quick 'once over' with a hound glove, followed by a polishing cloth and a bit of velvet will bring up breeds like Italian Greyhounds, Whippets and even Mastiffs looking just great. Of course in breeds such as Mastiffs and others that have some creases in their skin, for example the Pug, Bulldog and Shar-Pei, careful attention must be paid to these areas and a suitable moisturiser applied as necessary so that the skin does not dry out and become sore and unsightly. Bathing and frequency of bathing is very much a matter of personal preference and will vary according to the breed.

Wire Coats

Wire-haired coats, such as those found on many of the Terrier breeds, require an owner's time and skill to get them really looking good. Owning a show Terrier is quite a different matter from owning a pet that is simply taken to the grooming parlour every so often. Although it may come out looking neat and tidy, it will usually be a far cry from the carefully hand-stripped Terrier that wins top honours in the show ring. A typical Terrier coat requires a wiry, hard outer coat and a softer undercoat that is more dense, serving as a protection for the dog when working. To hand-strip a Terrier successfully can be likened to creating a living sculpture and anyone hoping to present such a breed for exhibition in the showring must have a very good eye, so that they know exactly what they are aiming for as an end result. Different groomers use different techniques and of course the quality of one's dog, as well as expertise in grooming, will play an important part in achieving success in the ring. It takes a long time to develop the skills to present certain breeds of Terrier to perfection, so I would strongly advise owners who are new to the showring to watch, listen and learn, and to be patient until they develop a thorough knowledge of their own breed.

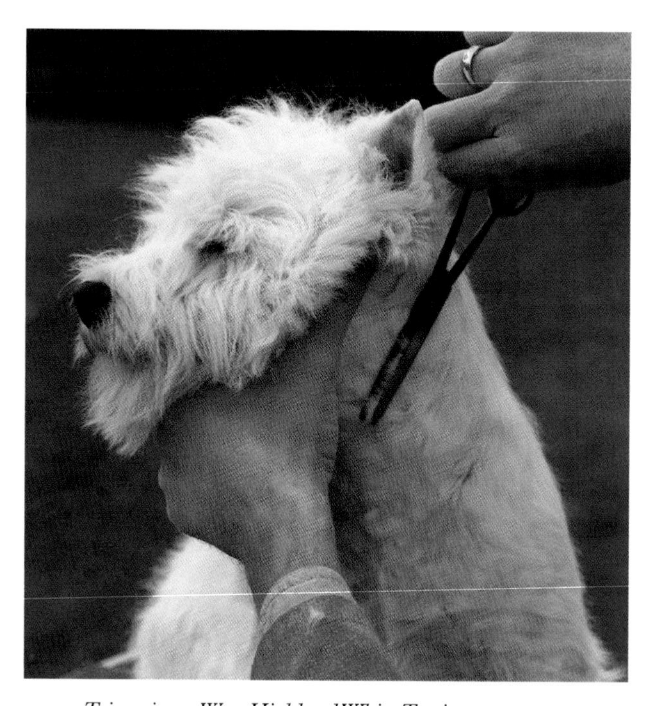

Trimming a West Highland White Terrier.

Long coats

What some people consider a long coat, others might think of as a relatively short one. There are major differences between the fairly long coat of an Irish Setter and the truly long coat of an Afghan Hound, Maltese or Shih Tzu. Each of these takes a different

Yorkie being put into protective coat after grooming – note this Yorkie has a tail, which is plaited for protection.

amount of work, and a different technique to get it looking really good. In long coated breeds bathing will be an integral part of the grooming process and in some breeds, even when groomed to perfection each and every week, it will take two or even three full hours to prepare a dog for a show the following day. Sometimes this can be done in advance, but this will depend on the breed, its coat texture and often even on the colour of the coat.

Some of the long-coated breeds can be trimmed just slightly, but in others trimming is simply not permitted. However, in most cases it is permissible to cut the coat growth from between the pads (under the foot) so there is no build up of coat which forms knots and can become painful. Many of the long-coated breeds are simply bathed and then groomed out thoroughly whilst drying is in progress, but other breeds, such as the Yorkshire Terrier, have the hair carefully folded in wraps to protect the ends and to encourage coat

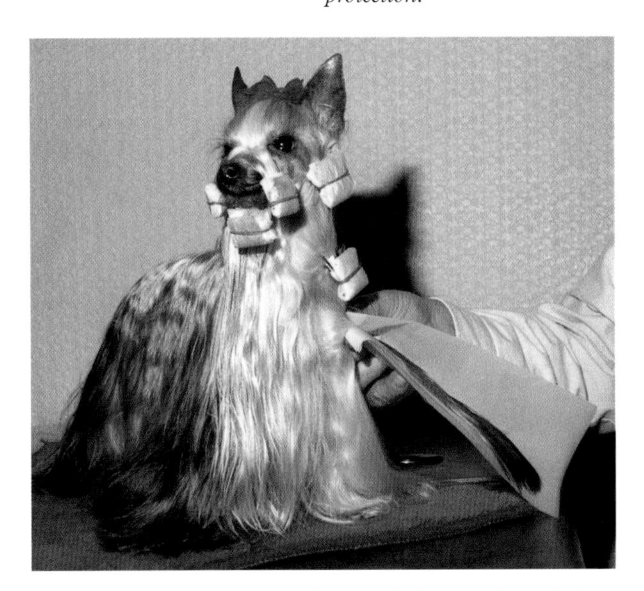

Carefully wrapping a Yorkie's coat after a bath.

Yorkie after grooming with coat now protected from damage.

growth. A Yorkshire Terrier can then be fitted with a neat little coat with trouser legs to further prevent damage. Yes, it's an enormous amount of time and trouble, but if you want a Yorkie that can win well in the showring such coat care is an absolute necessity. Just think of the pet Yorkies you see out in the street when you are shopping – honestly, do they really look much like those perfectly groomed, long-coated little gems that you see in the showring? I think not.

So when you look around the showring and see seasoned exhibitors constantly winning well, while as a newcomer you are maybe taking time to climb the tree, give a thought to the many years of dedication that have gone not only into careful breeding programmes, but also into coat preparation and skill in presenting it, as well as learning how to handle an exhibit to get the very best out of it in the ring.

I recall when Crufts used to be held in London and when I was showing Afghan Hounds on one day and Lhasa Apsos the next. I had to drive many miles home after the show on Hound day, bath my Apsos then turn tail and head back to London again without any sleep to exhibit on Utility Day the very next day. But I was not alone in doing this. There are many, many people out there who spend absolutely hours preparing their dogs and travelling to shows, sometimes coming back empty-handed, but at least we feel we have given it our best effort and have done our dogs proud!

CHAPTER 5

YOUR FIRST SHOW EXPERIENCE

Your very first show will come around all too soon and this will be an exciting day. You will have had to do lots of preparation in advance, not only will your dog have to be in tip-top condition, but you will have a million things to think about. As time goes on these will become a matter of course, but it takes time to get used to the dog showing routine so you should plan and be fairly methodical from the outset.

Before leaving home

Unless the show you are attending is a very local one, you will probably have to get up before dawn for an early start. If you have neighbours they probably won't appreciate you crashing around and slamming car doors so you should pack what you can in the car the night before. Not all shows begin at the same time, and not all breeds commence at the same time, but the 'start of judging' will be given either on the schedule or, in the case of a large Championship Show details will be sent out with your passes, and will probably also be listed in the weekly dog press. At a Championship Show, often one ring is used for more than one breed, so yours may be first, second or even third in the ring. Breeds for which CCs are on offer always have to take precedence over those without CCs, so if yours falls into the latter category, judging for you will usually commence a little later.

A hot day at an outdoor UK Championship Show.

You should also have remembered to fill up with petrol previously for many garages are not open until around 7a.m., and in any case you will probably want to get straight to the show without wasting time in a petrol station. You will also of course have planned the route to the show, always bearing in mind that you should allow extra time in case of congestion getting into the showground, especially if the dog show is combined with an agricultural event.

What you actually pack in the car will depend very much upon the breed you are showing; there may be a crate and a trolley or trolley-table and you will very probably want a 'space blanket' to reflect away the heat, especially if your dog is travelling in a crate. If yours is a large breed that is not crated you will need a benching chain so that your exhibit can be secured safely and easily to his bench. Being quite small this is easy to overlook and cannot always be purchased at a small show. Then of course there are essentials like collars and leads. You will probably be walking your dog out to the car on a fairly sturdy collar, but will you be using a show lead in the ring? If so, don't forget that either as you will have hopefully practised with it and although you will almost certainly be able to purchase another at the show, it may not be quite the same, so your new exhibit may not perform so well if wearing a different one.

Another essential is a plentiful supply of 'poo bags'. Pack some with your show gear and keep a couple handy in your pocket for when you arrive at the show.

Your own wet weather gear is something that could easily be packed in the car the night before, and sensible shoes or wellingtons are always handy to keep in the back of the

After a heavy downpour of rain, show organisers do all in their power to keep conditions underfoot as dry as possible, but nonetheless, Wellington boots are essential.

car in case the showground suffers a deluge and becomes like a quagmire. Believe me, it does happen, despite the show society's best laid plans! Maybe you also have wet weather gear for your dog, especially if you have a large, long-coated breed that is too heavy to carry, such as an Afghan Hound or Old English Sheepdog. If you haven't bought your dog's wet weather gear before your first show, you will certainly be able to find this at a Championship Show; usually it is a mackintosh with four legs and four separate waterproof 'shoes'. A couple of towels are also very handy to keep in the car, as is a kitchen roll, or perhaps two!

When you awake on the day of the show your dog will obviously need to be exercised and given the opportunity to relieve himself before setting off. You will feel much more comfortable in your own mind if you know he has 'been', so keep a careful eye on him so you will know what the score is when you finally get to the show. Rain, however light, and also early morning dew, can play havoc with a long-coated dog's appearance, so it is necessary to have planned how to handle this beforehand.

Obviously fresh water for your dog will have to be packed just before you leave, unless you are going to give him bottled water, in which case it could have been packed the night before. And if you are so well organised that you prepared a picnic the evening before, don't forget to take it out of the fridge and put it in the car, along with any liquid refreshment you may want for yourself. Undoubtedly taking a picnic to a show will be a cost saving and it also means that you will be able to stay with your dog all the while, instead of waiting in what are sometimes long food queues. Being with your dog will be particularly important at the start of your dog's show career, when he is not yet familiar with being left alone on a bench or in a crate.

Just a word of warning too, bearing in mind that you are probably leaving home at an unsociable hour. Be sure that your dog doesn't set off the car alarm by moving around in the car whilst you are still in the house collecting up the last few bits and pieces, or even getting yourself changed into your showing outfit. Some people, by the way, opt to travel in something casual and take an outfit into which to change at the show. Occasionally it is quite remarkable seeing the difference in someone's appearance when they enter the ladies' loo and then re-appear from the cubicle in smart jacket and trousers! But be warned, not all lavatories of the portable variety are conducive to changing one's outfit.

A travelling companion?

Perhaps you are travelling to a show with a companion, which can always make a long journey seem shorter as time passes more quickly if you are chatting as you drive along. And when you have become ensconced in the dog world, I promise you there will be lots to chat about!

When travelling with someone, especially if your companion, too, is taking a dog to the show, you will have to plan the packing of your car very carefully, for you don't want to find yourself in a position of having to bail out your own dog to let the other one in. Or of course there may be several. And of course the dogs must be transported in the safest possible way, ideally in a crate so that if by chance you have an accident whilst travelling, the dogs cannot escape and run into the traffic. On the other hand, the dogs must at all times be easily accessible, so that they can be taken out if necessary, and offered water if thirsty. There is, by the way, a dog's drinking bowl that is designed so that it doesn't spill; this is ideal for leaving inside a crate whilst the car is in motion.

Finding the right car park

Usually dog shows are fairly well signposted within the last few miles of approaching the venue, and if you are travelling to a small show there will probably be only one car park, so you will have no problem provided you can find a spot, which is not always easy if you don't arrive early. However, if you are going to a large all-breed Championship Show there may be several different car parks and the one you need will be the one closest to your judging ring. In most cases, car park tickets will be posted out to you in advance and the one in which you are to park will be colour designated. This means it is essential to know exactly where your car park pass is before you get to the show for often the car park entrances are on completely different roads leading into the venue.

Also at a few shows, such as those held at the National Exhibition Centre near Birmingham, the car parks are so widespread that shuttle buses are in operation to transport you to the venue itself, all the more reason to have been absolutely methodical in your packing.

Should you have a disabled badge you may not be allowed to use the disabled car park unless you have applied in advance to the show society for a pass for that specific area. To do this you will probably have to send in a copy of your disabled badge with your show entry. This is not the case at every show, but more and more shows are now organising facilities in this way to prevent the system being abused, thereby causing the disabled car park to become so full that genuinely registered disabled exhibitors have to be turned away to park elsewhere.

Locating your benching area

Having remembered very carefully where you parked your vehicle, unloaded your goods and shackles and made your way to the show entrance with your dog, at a major Championship Show you will probably have to present your pass, allowing your dog into the exhibition area. Keep this handy at all times as you will also need part of it when you leave.

You will also usually be able to collect your pre-paid catalogue from a booth near the entrance. If you are lucky, a helpful member of the show's organising committee will take a quick look at your breed and point you in the right direction for your benching area. If not, the ring numbers will be listed in the front of your catalogue and it is likely that you will also have been sent a plan of the show's layout with your passes. Yet another good reason for keeping all those pieces of paper safe.

Each bench is given a number and now your aim will be to find the bench with the same number as that given on your pass. It sounds easy but is not always so, for at some shows, for some inexplicable reason best known to the organisers, not all numbers run in

The benching and exhibition area of an indoor Championship Show.

consecutive order. Anyway, sooner or later you will have found your bench and if you have a large dog this will certainly be your base for the day. Indeed it will technically be your base whatever size of breed you have, but if you have a breed that needs to be groomed up at the show, such as a Poodle, Lhasa Apso or Maltese, you will usually find that a grooming area has been designated reasonably close to the judging ring. However, if you don't arrive at the show early, you may not find a space here, or you may indeed prefer to groom your dog up at your benching area if you have only one dog.

If you are attending a benched show, you will most probably find two copies of your ring number waiting on your bench. One must remain there, the other is the one that you will wear in the ring so you will attach this to your ring clip, or insert into the transparent pocket in your armband. Remember that the judge will not be allowed to judge your dog until you are displaying your number, so don't lose it.

At an Open Show, you may have to collect your ring number from the Secretary's table when you arrive at the show, or it may be given out to you by the steward in the ring. If you are unsure, just make an enquiry when you arrive at the show so that you are not caught out without your number when your class begins.

Also at an Open show, or indeed a breed club show, it is unlikely that your dog will be benched, so you will keep your dog with you all day. If yours is a small dog you will most probably wish to keep it mainly in a crate, but if larger you should take along a dog blanket to place on the floor so that your dog is as comfortable as possible at the show.

Practicalities at the show

If you are attending a benched show, or if your dog is crated, you should be able to leave your dog for a few moments whilst you visit the lavatory and get refreshments, but always be sure that you ask someone to keep an eye on your dog whilst you are away. Clearly it is much easier if you travel to a show with a friend, relation or travelling companion, for you can always take it in turns to look after your dog or dogs. If you are travelling alone, you will have to be dependent on people who are located close to you, but as time goes on you will get to know your regular neighbours quite well. At a major show at which each dog exhibited has a bench allocated to it (known as a 'benched show'), ring numbers are placed on the top of each bench. These numbers are always issued according to the alphabetical order of exhibitors within that breed, so for example, if Whippet owner Mrs Y Smallwood is number 1000, Whippet owner Mrs J Smith will be 1001 and Mrs T Smith will be 1002 and so on. As a result, if you are campaigning your dog in Scotland or at Bournemouth on the south coast, those people benched next to you will be roughly the same if they have travelled to that specific show.

The toilet blocks are not always as conveniently located as you might wish, so if you are passing a block on your way into the show it is probably a good idea to call off there as you arrive, if of course it is safe to leave your dogs. You will have taken some fresh water for your dog, but on a hot day you may need a refill. If using the water in the toilet block, be sure you are getting water from a tap marked 'drinking water'. At large outdoor shows there are usually a few standpipes located around the show ground, so you can fill up there, and on a hot day it is not at all unusual to see a dog refreshing itself with a drink as the water flows freely. Such taps are very useful for cooling a dog down with water when the weather is hot.

Heat is a very important thing to consider at a show, especially if you have a breed that needs to be groomed and you therefore need to position your grooming table when you arrive. Many people have umbrellas attached to the side of the grooming table and this will certainly help, but the most effective method is to choose a spot in the shade. Keep in mind that the sun will travel round during the course of the day so always think ahead. Please don't choose a nice sunny spot in which you can do your own personal bit of sunbathing; at a dog show it is always your dog that is most important and it is essential that he is kept comfortable throughout the day.

As some small measure of keeping down the temperature in a dog's crate you may decide to buy a little specially made fan that can be attached to the outside, thus circulating the air inside. These don't cost a great deal and can usually be found on sale at large shows. Other people, especially with small short-nosed (brachcycephalic) breeds use an ice-pack under the bedding in the bottom of the crate.

Another very useful piece of equipment is a space blanket, which I have already mentioned for use in your car. This usually has a dark coloured material on one side and silver on the reverse. If hot you use the silver side outermost (vice versa if you want to keep your dog warm) and this reflects away the heat. They can be used draped over dog or crate, or can now be found actually designed to fits crates, with useful pockets in the sides. These I find a veritable godsend for my own small dogs. It is also now possible to buy dog

A show official measuring the temperature inside a car. It is important to realise that temperatures can rise incredibly quickly, even with the back open and a space blanket in place.

This important notice speaks for itself.

coats made of the same combination and I am sure these are very useful, especially for larger dogs.

Unless you are absolutely certain of the weather conditions for the entire day, make sure to take gear for all eventualities with you into the showground. Car parks can be a good distance away, and it is no good discovering around lunchtime that you really did need your space blanket, fan, umbrella or wellington boots when they are packed safely in your car maybe twenty minutes' walk, or even further away.

At some early point in the day, you will of course have exercised your dog on a lead, giving him the opportunity to relieve himself before going into the ring. At most shows exercise areas are clearly designated, so please be sure to use these. It is essential that you clean up after your dog, so always keep a 'poo bag' handy. This can be tied up and disposed of easily in the next available waste area, sometimes just a strategically positioned black bag. Poo bags come in all colours; at shows you can buy special green or black ones, even with a cardboard scoop attached, but you will probably find it more economical to buy nappy bags from your local chemist.

On a more savoury subject (as a dog person, you will find you can talk about absolutely anything in virtually the same breath), earlier I mentioned taking a picnic to a show. This is actually a very good idea if you are the sort of person who is organised well enough to do so.

Personally, I just throw a couple of bananas into my grooming bag and then spend ages waiting in food queues. Certainly plenty of food is on offer at most shows and I have to admit that on a cold day it is nice to get something hot inside you, but at smaller show, such as some leisure centres, hot food is often cooked to order so the waiting time can seem endless.

At large Championship Shows, food stalls are located around the perimeter of the showground, often with several similar stalls placed together, which is convenient because you can look around first of all to see what food you fancy. In such situations the queuing time is usually shorter, but the prices are pretty high so don't be surprised if you have to part with more than a five-pound note for a sandwich and a cup of tea. Unless you have someone looking after your dog, you will then have to carry your purchases back to your bench, or wherever your dog is situated. So even if you are fortunate enough to have been provided with a plastic cover for your tea, it will probably be tepid by the time you drink it and your bacon butty or hot potato with chilli filling will be stone cold!

Wet weather accommodation

At all large shows and at most smaller ones too, societies make some provision for judging to take place under cover if necessary. Obvious circumstances under which this happens are heavy rain and particularly strong winds, but sometimes although it may not be raining overhead the ground underfoot is sodden due to a recent spate of heavy downpours. Some breeds and their enthusiasts seem hardier than others, for often just a few of the larger breeds will opt to be judged outside whilst the rest of their canine fraternity seeks shelter.

Using wet weather accommodation is rarely as pleasant as being judged outside and also it can vary tremendously according to the show. At agricultural centres, cattle sheds are used and some of these are not too bad at all, whilst others can get bitterly cold. In many cases extra tenting is provided alongside the areas allocated for dogs' benching but this is usually very cramped and rarely provides the most pleasurable day for judge, exhibitors, onlookers or dogs. There is rarely much space around the ring, so it is difficult to follow what is going on in the judging area and if the wind is strong, tent flaps have a very nasty habit of flapping enthusiastically and frightening dogs. Tents have even been known to blow down in the wind, but show officials are always on the alert for this and take as many precautionary measures as possible.

A few of the large show societies in Britain use a very elaborate form of tenting, designed such that the benching areas are inside and the showing areas are partly covered and partly open, so that in poor weather conditions it simply means that a smaller area of the ring is utilised. This avoids the necessity of everyone having to make a dash to the designated covered ring when the heavens open, as so often seems to happen. Frequently a judge commences judging a breed outside in the hope that any threatening storm clouds will pass over, but if they don't it's a major upheaval to get everything under cover quickly, especially dogs that are crated.

At major shows when judging moves under cover it usually remains there, but at smaller shows where the conditions are often very cramped, judging can move inside and out several times in one day. Thankfully camaraderie in the dog showing world is first rate and even on the wettest day exhibitors and dogs can still thoroughly enjoy their day out.

Juliette Cunliffe taking a final look at a Shih Tzu Puppy Class, before selecting her winners.

Things to Think About

How much can I pack in the car the night before the show?

Fill up with petrol.

Should I travel with a companion, or not?

Don't forget the wet weather gear.

Plan also for hot weather.

Planning the route and heading for the right car park.

Remembering exactly where I parked the car.

Studying the show information to locate my breed.

CHAPTER 6

PREPARING FOR YOUR ENTRANCE INTO THE RING

Whatever breed of dog you are taking to the show, you will always need to give yourself and your dog time to settle down upon arrival at the show. Few dogs will cope well with being rushed from the car and hurried straight into the ring, so make sure you allow yourself plenty of time to get to the area of your dog's ring and show bench. If separate sexes are classified, such as at a breed show or general Championship Show, males, known as dogs, are always judged before bitches, and the puppy classes are usually first (sometimes preceded by Veteran), so if you have a young dog you need to arrive especially early.

How much you will have to set up when you get to your benching or grooming area will depend largely on the breed of dog you have. If you have a Whippet a quick once over with a chamois leather or piece of velvet should be all you need. On this subject something called a hound glove is a very useful piece of grooming equipment for it is a kind of mitten that fits onto your hand, with soft chamois leather on one side to use first, and velvet on the other just to give that final gleam to the coat.

Setting up your grooming table

Every exhibitor has some personal preference as to what they use as equipment at a show. Some exhibitors, even with large dogs that need preparation before entering the ring, take along a trolley on which the dog can stand to be groomed. In such cases usually the dog will be walked into the showground from the car park, possibly wearing some footwear so that the feet don't get dirty, especially on a wet day. So the kind of table that is most popular for a large dog is one that doubles as a trolley so that this heavy item doesn't have to be carried into the show. It is also useful for transporting anything you may be taking into the showground besides your dog.

Small dogs, especially coated ones, are generally taken into the showground in crates, the crates being placed either on top of a trolley or specially made so that they double as a table, with a grooming surface on the top.

All these items of equipment can be purchased at a major show and although they will be quite pricey, if chosen carefully they will give many a long year of good service. If you have more than one dog that needs to be crated you could be well advised to have separate crates for each dog. This is not a necessity, but getting one single dog out of a crate at a show is easier than taking one out and leaving another one or two inside. The latter may just decide they want to come too and you might possibly have an escape on your hands!

I have already mentioned that at some larger shows and at breed shows, grooming areas are usually designated somewhere near the ringside. Show societies appreciate that exhibitors with more than one dog often find it virtually impossible to rush back to the bench to return a dog and then hurry back to the ring with another; all this takes time and delays judging. But wherever you decide to set up your own grooming table, you must be certain that gangways are not obstructed. All shows must adhere to strict security regulations in case of fire and such like, so all exits and gangways must be kept free. If you decide to set up your grooming equipment somewhere where it obviously shouldn't be, you will almost certainly be moved on by a show official, which can be very inconvenient if you have finished unpacking everything.

If your crate and table are separate, you may decide to put your crate on the bench and the table in front of it, but again take care not to obstruct the gangway between the benches and always show consideration to your neighbours. Occasionally the benches are smaller than you would like, but under no circumstances remove partitions between the benches. Not only is this strictly not allowed, but it can affect the stability of the entire row and could cause an accident.

Benching a larger dog

If you have a large dog its bench will be its 'home' for the day, so make this as comfortable as possible. Take along some soft bedding, such as veterinary bedding or a soft quilt, for benches are made of wood, sometimes metal and wood, so can be very hard. At the back of the bench you will find a steel loop, to which you should attach one end of your benching chain. The other end will be attached to your dog's substantial collar. Under no circumstances attach this to a show lead; the show lead will be put on before entering the ring. Take care that the benching chain is the right length for your dog, so that he cannot step off the bench; conversely he must not be chained too tightly.

Because there is rarely any benching at an Open Show, exhibitors have to set up their own grooming areas if they are to present their dogs to perfection. (CUNLIFFE)

Hopefully you will stay with your dog all the time at the show or, if not, you will leave him under the care and supervision of someone you know and trust. All being well, your dog's temperament will be utterly sound, but if you are at all unsure you would be well advised to put some protection in front of the bench so that people and other dogs are not tempted to approach too closely. We should always remember that it is a dog's duty to protect, and a dog on his bench considers this his own private space and may be more protective than he might otherwise be. Most other show people will of course know how to treat another person's dog on a bench, but at shows that attract numerous members of the public, such as Crufts, exhibitors should be especially aware that all sorts of fingers may be poked at a dog on his bench and that this will not always be appreciated.

Having said that, there is absolutely no excuse for bad temperament and a dog that is of unsound or unreliable temperament should not be shown. In fact if there is an incident and it is reported to the Show Secretary and hence the KC, it is unlikely that the dog will be permitted to be shown again.

Socialising your dog

When you have sorted yourself out and settled into your chosen spot, you would be well advised to allow your dog to stretch his legs and relieve himself if he likes. This will give him an opportunity to absorb the atmosphere of the show and to take in the sights, sounds and smells that surround him.

Don't allow him to be over-friendly with other dogs for they, or their owners, may not appreciate his youthful enthusiasm. Usually you will be able to find a fairly quiet spot where you can practise moving your dog at the sort of speed you will be moving him in the ring – this will give both of you a little more confidence and you will have some idea of how he is likely to perform a little later on in the day.

At breed shows that take place at an indoor venue, there is usually no objection to exhibitors practising in the ring for a moment or two before judging gets underway. This gives the dogs, especially the young ones, a chance to get a feel for the floor's surface which is probably covered in matting with which they will be unfamiliar. However, don't overdo it and be sure to vacate the ring as soon as the judge appears on the horizon.

Presentation of your dog before entering the ring

Because there are so many breeds of dogs, and because virtually each of them is presented in a slightly different way, it would be impossible to go into detail about how to groom them all. Suffice it to say, you will hopefully have been given sound advice from the breeder of your show dog, you will have read books about your breed and you will have had an opportunity to purchase most, if not all, your grooming equipment well before the show.

Almost certainly when you have been to a few shows and have watched other people preparing their dogs, you will pick up tips – either offered, or of which you have taken a mental note – and sooner or later you will find yourself around the stalls buying a few non-essential extras. Soon enough they will probably have become 'essentials' for you will do all in your power to present your dog to perfection, and if something works well on your own dog's coat, it is well worth spending the money.

At this European show some exhibitors have even taken along their hairdryers to put the final touches. Note also that instead of a benching area, large crates are set up at floor level. (CUNLIFFE)

As time goes on you will have got to know which shampoos and conditioners suit best, and when you have decided on the ones you really like it is worth investing in large sized bottles which will give you much more value for money. Most stalls now accept credit cards by the way.

The sprays you use on your dog's coat at a show must fall within the KC's 'Regulations for the Preparation of Dogs for Exhibition'. These are quite strict and can result in disciplinary action by the KC if not adhered to. So that these rules cannot be misconstrued I quote:

> *a) No substance which alters the natural colour, texture or body of the coat may be present in the dog's coat for any purpose at any time during the Show. No substance which alters the natural colour of any external part of the dog may be present on the dog for any purpose at any time during the Show.*
> *b) Any other substance (other than water) which may be used in the preparation of a dog for exhibition must not be allowed to remain in the coat or on any other part of the dog at the time of exhibition.*

It is always worth keeping in the back of your mind that the KC's General Committee may, without notice, order an examination of any dog or dogs at any Show.

Obviously what you use in the preparation of your dog's coat at home, between shows, is a matter of personal choice, so long as the colour is not changed and that it is removed from the coat for exhibition. Indeed many owners use various preparations on their dogs' coats between shows, such as those that prevent hair breakage and those that help avoid tangles forming in the coat. At any show you will find the people who man the grooming and equipment stalls very helpful, and they should be able to offer you sound advice as to what you can and cannot safely use.

When and when not to make acquaintances and ask advice

In general when you first start showing your dog you will find that many people are helpful, but when you start beating their dogs in the showring their attitude may just change. This is not always the case but it can happen, so this is just a word of warning. Some breeds are said to be more welcoming to newcomers than others, so let's hope your own breed is one of the former.

As I have already mentioned, many people are willing to give advice if you ask, but do choose the moment of your enquiry with care. No exhibitor wants to be bombarded with questions just before he or she is about to take a dog into the ring. Just to be on the safe side, you could always preface your question by, 'Is now the right time for me to ask you about ...?' Most people will tell you quite straightforwardly that it's fine to do so, or suggest a better time, such as 'Not just now. Catch me when I've come out of Limit Bitch, if you don't mind.' Don't take offence; what they say will be in everyone's best interests if the timing is right.

Many newcomers to the showring are just bursting to ask questions of the judge, but really that is not in order. I remember being confronted in the ladies loo by an unhappy exhibitor whose dog I had not placed. She had clearly been waiting for me to come out of the cubicle and got me whilst I was washing my hands. Exhibitors must remember that judges have probably judged over two hundred dogs in a day, so to remember the details of each and every one, when the dog is not in front of them, is almost asking the impossible.

If for some reason a judge approaches you about your dog when judging is completed, that's quite another matter. It may be that the judge has seen potential in your dog and wants to offer advice as to how you can get the best out of him. However, in many cases judges' and exhibitors' time is at a premium at a show, so don't be despondent if you get 'thrown out' of a class and no-one commiserates.

It is generally considered unethical to have close encounters with your judge immediately prior to show day, even though you might know the judge well. And certainly don't offer to give your judge a lift to the show. Believe me, it has been done! Nor will a judge appreciate an exhibitor ringing him the night before the show, maybe to tell the judge what a wonderful new puppy he has, or to ask what time judging starts. If you have a genuine question about the time your breed is expected in the ring and cannot find an answer in the schedule, by all means telephone the secretary a few days prior to the show, but not the night before please as he or she is certain to have far too much to do by way of preparation for the show.

Overseas attitudes are a little more relaxed about communication immediately prior to a show. I have been on many a judging engagement abroad where I have been invited to an official dinner the night before the show, only to find my table partners exhibiting under me the next day. I have even had meals the night before a show with the next day's exhibits sitting at my feet under the table. Also, on many occasions I have had a sudden change of steward, only to find that the one I had been working with all day is standing there in the line up with her dog for the next class!

You will see that the etiquette of being a good exhibitor does indeed vary from country to country, so all I can really say is 'When in Rome, do as the Romans'.

Things to Think About

Secure my dog safely at the show.

Give him opportunity to relieve himself.

Carry 'poo' bags at all times.

Practise moving before entering the ring.

Prepare my dog to look good in the ring.

Only ask questions at the right time.

Be sure I have my ring number ready for display.

Be sure someone will keep an eye on my dog when I'm away.

At most shows exhibits in adjacent rings are in close proximity to one another, so dogs have to be kept well under control and be on their best behaviour. Here this Tibetan Mastiff is being judged in a ring adjacent to Rottweilers.

CHAPTER 7

YOU AND YOUR DOG ARE IN THE RING

The big moment has arrived and you are about to enter the ring with your dog. Don't be surprised if you are feeling a little nervous; most people feel like that at the beginning. To alleviate your personal fears, always keep in the back of your mind that the judge and the ringside will be looking at your dog, not at you. You really must try to remain as calm as possible, for any tension you are feeling will travel dog to your dog and he, too, will share your anxiety and not perform so well as he might otherwise do.

Going into the ring

Be sure that you and your dog are fully prepared before the start of judging of your class. Keep an eye on what is happening in the class before you, so that you can be waiting patiently by the ringside for a few moments before you go in. You will at some point have found a few moments to watch the procedure this judge is using. Does he move the class around the ring before individual assessment? If so, how many times? And what pattern of movement will he expect from you and your dog? If you have taken note of these things before you go in, you will be better prepared to concentrate fully on your dog.

You will need to keep your mind as clear as possible in the ring, so make sure you will not worry about what you may or may not have left visible on your bench. Obviously you can't take your handbag into the ring, so make sure it has been left with someone for safe-keeping. And don't take your mobile 'phone into the ring unless it is switched off and safely tucked inside your pocket. Use of mobile telephones inside the ring, and indeed in the general vicinity of the ring is not acceptable.

If this is a show at which numbers are not given out in the ring, also be sure that you are wearing your ring number (the correct one of course) for you will not want the steward to have to send you out of the ring to collect it from your bench before you can be judged. That may just throw you into a panic and you will not have time to set up your dog properly before judging commences.

Just occasionally a judge will request that all exhibits in the ring are lined up in numerical order, in which case you will have no choice as to exactly where you stand and unless you like to be first, you may wish your family name wasn't Abbot as ring numbers are always related to the alphabetical order of exhibitors within a breed. However, in most cases exhibitors will all enter roughly together and find their own place. As a novice

This highly successful St Bernard is being moved at the correct pace to show off all its attributes in the Best in Show ring.

exhibitor, it is probably unwise to land up at the beginning of the line, nor is it a good idea to be last as you will have very little time to get your dog looking perfect for the judge when he makes his final appraisal. You would probably be best advised to find a spot somewhere in the middle, but certainly don't push your way in, just plan your timing as you enter the ring. You may also wish to consider which dogs you prefer not to stand next to. If yours is on the small side, you would be better avoiding a particularly large dog, for example. If yours is a coated breed and your own dog is not yet in full coat, you would be wiser not to stand next to a dog that is dripping in coat and groomed to perfection.

If you know that a certain exhibitor is a particular chatterbox, try to avoid standing next to her in the ring. Outside the ring is the place for chatting at length, not inside. While exhibiting your dog you will need to concentrate one hundred per cent on the job in hand. That means keeping a careful eye on your dog, and another on the judge.

Although your dog should be allowed the opportunity to relax whilst not being individually assessed by the judge, take care that he does not stand in some particularly awkward, unattractive position. Often a judge will cast a quick eye around the ring between exhibits, just to refresh his or her memory of those already seen, so you don't want your dog to be caught out not looking his best. You should also remember that there is a ringside audience and some of the people who are watching may perhaps be judging in a few weeks' time.

When it is your dog's turn to be assessed you will move from your place along the edge of the ring to the centre, or if you have a 'table dog', you will place the dog on the table so that he looks as good as he can whilst the previous exhibitor is moving his dog. Under no circumstances cross in front of the judge, nor should you cause an obstruction in any way, either to the judge or the exhibit being assessed.

Present your dog as best you can, but never let go of the lead whilst the judge is going over him, for you must always be in control of your exhibit. On the other hand, don't get in the way of the judge by holding your dog's head firmly while the judge is trying to go

This exhibitor is attracting her Japanese Shiba Inu's attention from the front, so that it stands exactly as the judge would like to see it.

A still wrinkly Shar-Pei puppy getting used to being handled by the judge at its very first Championship Show.

over it. Although not obliged to, the judge will generally ask the age of your dog, so make sure you've worked that out before you go in the ring. He will usually start by assessing your dog's head, at which time, in the vast majority of breeds, he will want to inspect the teeth and bite. Most judges will do this themselves, but some prefer to ask the exhibitor to show the teeth, so you should know how to do this before you go to a show. Unless you have a Shar-Pei or Chow Chow (in which case more aspects of the inside of the mouth will be looked at), the judge will be principally interested in the placement of the teeth, the shape of the jaw and how the upper and lower jaws close together. So if you do find yourself in the position of being asked to show the teeth, remember to keep your dog's mouth closed. Actually if you feel your dog is a little 'mouth shy', you may ask the judge's permission that you show the teeth, instead of the judge looking himself.

The judge will then work to the back of the body, and in the case of a male will check for testicles. Hopefully your dog will have two, but if for veterinary reasons they have been removed and the KC has been duly notified, always keep a copy of the veterinary letter in your pocket for the judge should ask to see this. Finally the judge will ask you to move your dog. Here I should mention that there are some differences in the way certain breeds are judged, the Pekingese being a prime example. Usually a judge will not look inside the mouth of a Pekingese (nor of a Pug) and will pick up the dog himself to assess the weight. The Pekingese is also a breed that is shown facing the judge, rather than in profile, as are some other breeds such as the Bulldog and Staffordshire Bull Terrier.

Other breeds, the Miniature and Toy Poodle and German Spitz Mittel and Klein are measured by the judge when on the table. This may seem a little off-putting for you as an exhibitor at first, but your dog will become very used to this and provided that the judge is experienced in using the wicket adeptly, your dog will not bat an eyelid. Another breed that is measured is the Miniature Dachshund (all three varieties), but for this breed the measurement is for weight. Scales will have been placed on the table at the beginning of each class and the judge will watch whilst each dog is weighed. You will occasionally notice an exhibitor taking off the dog's lead before going on the scales – if a dog is toward the upper weight limit, every ounce counts!

This lovely Yorkshire Terrier has been groomed to absolute perfection, but an enormous amount of care and attention is needed to grow the coat to this length and to keep it in such tip-top condition.

Are you a 'seen' dog?

When you first enter the ring the steward will probably indicate that 'new' dogs are to be on one side and 'seen' dogs on another. New dogs are those that have not been assessed by this particular judge at the show, seen dogs are those that have.

If the steward is a good one, he will arrange for the seen dogs to stand in the order in which they have been placed. So if, for example, you won third in Puppy, but the second prize winner in Puppy is also a seen dog in the same class, that dog will stand ahead of you. However, there may be other dogs that have been placed but which your own dog has not met. These dogs also will be grouped together according to their wins in their respective classes. This the steward will most probably explain to the judge (though the judge should actually remember in what order he has placed the dogs of course) and he will compare dogs that have been seen in one class with those that have been seen in another.

He is unlikely to fully appraise each seen dog again unless there is something he particularly wants to check. Usually he will move some or all of them again individually, but is under no obligation to do so. It is also likely that he will ask them all then to join onto the end of the line of new dogs so that he can stand back and take a look at them all together for comparison's sake, following which he will place the winners, including one or more of the seen dogs, as he sees fit.

Moving your dog

You will have watched the way the other exhibitors have moved their dogs, but the judge will tell you briefly what is expected. The direction in which he requires you to move your

Handlers need to adjust their own pace to suit the size of dog they are exhibiting, in this case a Chihuahua.

exhibit will depend to a certain extent upon the shape of the ring, but he will be aiming to see your dog's movement from the front, from the back and in profile.

If you are in a small indoor venue it is possible that there is just one rubber mat placed centrally across the ring, in which case the most usual request will be to move your dog up and down twice. The first time the judge will stand at the end of the mat so he can assess your dog 'coming' and 'going'. Then he will move to the side of the mat to assess the movement in profile. Whilst in general you should always move your dog on your left hand side, if the ring is shaped like this and the judge is standing at the side of the mat, in one direction you will have to change so that your dog moves on your right, so as not to obstruct the judge's view. This is something you will have to have practised prior to the show.

In fact under no circumstances should you ever obstruct the judge's view of your dog, which means that when you turn at the end of the ring you should move around your dog, not in front of him. Regrettably you will see many people do exactly the reverse, either because they know no better, or because they feel their dog turns better that way, but strictly speaking you should try never to get between your dog and the judge.

The substantially built Bloodhound is shown with its tail held up to show it off to best advantage.

This Irish Setter is being presented perfectly by its owner, with head and tail held at just the correct levels.

In a larger ring, you will most probably be asked to move in a triangle (again keeping your dog on your left hand side) and then either up and down, or sometimes back to the end of the line of dogs by way of an arc, thus giving the judge another opportunity to assess profile movement. If the judge is using the latter method, which incidentally is used most frequently on the Continent, he may initially ask you just to move up and down, not in a triangle. Whichever way you are asked to move, you must follow the judge's strict instructions. If he wants a straight line, be sure you do just that; if a triangle, make nice clean corners as you turn. There is nothing more frustrating for a judge than to find that an exhibitor does something completely different from that which has been requested!

Each judge will have their own personal preference as to what they expect of you, the exhibitor. Many will expect you to stand your dog for him to see after having been moved, but this is not always the case as the judge will have another opportunity to see the dogs standing in line as the end of the class. If you are asked to stand your dog after moving, you will find that some judges like the dog to be allowed to free stand, so will not want you to actually stack him.

Standing or stacking your dog

Different breeds are presented in different ways, and even within a breed exhibitors have

Lhasa Apsos, like all smaller breeds, are presented on a table for individual assessment by the judge.

their own preference as to which way they like to show them. In some breeds, especially the smaller ones, people bend down behind their dogs and place the feet in the correct position with their hands, in some cases, just supporting the tail so that it remains in exactly the right position. If necessary they will also just support the neck and head of the dog (without the hand showing of course) so that it is held in just the right place. This is called 'stacking' a dog. However, in the very same breed, some people prefer to stand up and have trained their dogs to stand exactly as they want them to. This can sometimes be the case if the exhibitor has some difficulty bending or kneeling down, but sometimes it is just because they prefer to show in this way.

Free standing is the method used for many of the larger breeds, when the exhibitors train the dog to walk into the correct position so that the legs are positioned in exactly the best place to do justice to the dog. This is frequently done by way of baiting, so as to attract the dog's attention. Usually female exhibitors wear a little bag around the waist in which the bait is kept, though men tend to use their pockets; small pieces are taken out with the effect of drawing the dog's attention, so that his neck is positioned well too. In certain breeds such as the Rottweiler, Dobermann and Shar Pei for example, this is an accepted method of showing and obtains the desired results. However I would urge exhibitors not to attempt to feed a dog bait exactly when the judge is trying to assess the head, as this can be infuriating for the judge in question!

As I mentioned earlier, sometimes, upon its return after moving, a judge will expect a dog to free stand, even if it is a breed that is usually stacked, so do watch the exhibitors before you so that you know what is expected of you when it comes to your own turn.

Keeping an eye on the judge

Although your most important concern in the ring is the presentation and behaviour of your dog, it is also incredibly important that you keep an eye on the judge, especially at the beginning and end of each class.

Although there is a recommended speed of judging, judges invariably do things in slightly different ways. Some take more time at the judge's table, some tend to cast an eye across the ring as the exhibits are brought in but almost invariably at the beginning of each

This high quality Staffordshire Bull Terrier is being presented perfectly for the cameras following a very rewarding win at a major Championship Show.

class, they will take a walk up and down the ring to look at the exhibits before moving them all together and then assessing them individually. Usually they will move all the dogs around together at the beginning of a breed class, and in large classes they may even divide the dogs into two groups for moving, so that they have ample space to stride out. In mixed breed classes the judge is less likely to move all the dogs around together, largely because of their different sizes and speeds at which they would move.

It is absolutely essential that your dog is presented to perfection from the very outset. This is the time to concentrate on your dog, not to get into deep conversation with the exhibitor next to you. If your dog is not ready at the beginning of the class, if you have not kept your eye on the judge so that you know exactly when he is moving away from the judge's table to take his initial look around the class, you may just have thrown away a chance of success. Many an experienced judge will take a quick mental note of the dogs he thinks he likes at the very beginning of the class, and will confirm his initial appraisal upon individual assessment. Those he has not taken a mental note of initially, may just have to pull out even more stops to make him appreciate their merits when he is going over them and watching them move.

When the class is in progress you should also keep a careful eye on the judge as I mentioned earlier, for many a good judge will cast a quick eye around the ring between exhibits. I do this myself, mentally making my rough placings of the dogs I like as I go along.

Judge, Liz Stannard, takes a careful look around the dogs exhibited in a variety class, where various different breeds are in competition with each other.

Liz Stannard approaching to make her assessment of this Dobermann, whilst other exhibitors await their turn.

The Bulldog is one of a handful of breeds that is shown head-on to the judge. But a judge will usually also walk around the dog to view it from the side, rear and from above to clearly asses its body shape.

Very occasionally a judge will actually slot dogs into the places he sees fit, after assessment of each dog. He is perfectly within his rights to do this, but it is not usually a method favoured by exhibitors, especially not for those who find themselves placed further and further down the line as the class progresses. When using this particular method of judging, which I reiterate is unusual in the UK, the judge will generally move all the dogs again at the end of the class and even assess some of them again briefly, then possibly changing some of the places before the awards are made.

At the very end of the class the judge (unless using the latter method) will walk up and down the line of dogs in order to select those he wishes to place. He may move some of the dogs again, but not necessarily all, so be sure you watch to see whether or not he wants you to move your own dog. He might also go over some points on some or even all of the dogs again. In many cases he will come up to the dogs in line, but in Toy breeds and Tibetan Spaniels, for example, exhibitors prefer a judge to see their dogs again on the table, rather than on the floor, so if you have one of these breeds, don't be taken aback if you are asked to put your dog on the table again.

Another possibility you may encounter is that the judge will want to see two dogs moving together. This is usually because he cannot quite decide between the two for two of the placings. Again, another reason to keep your wits always about you to be sure you know what is expected of you and your dog.

Things to Think About

Keep a general eye on what's happening in the ring.

Put my valuable possessions somewhere safe.

How is the judge moving the dogs?

Where shall I stand when I enter the ring?

Don't allow my dog to stand in an ungainly position.

Remember not to leave my comb on the floor or table.

Remember never to obstruct the judge's view.

Always keep an eye on the judge.

CHAPTER 8

PROBLEMS YOU MIGHT ENCOUNTER

Even the most experienced exhibitor can occasionally encounter a mishap in the ring, but as a new exhibitor you are more likely to be put off by such things, not knowing quite how to handle the situation for the best.

Forgotten your ring number or wearing the wrong one

I have already stressed the importance of remembering to collect your ring number from the bench, and of course that the number you collect is the correct one. It is usually the steward who checks off exhibitors' ring numbers before judging starts in each class, so it will be at this moment that you realise your unfortunate mistake, for the judge is not allowed to judge your dog unless you are wearing the correct number.

With luck you will have a friend by the ringside who will make a mad dash over to the bench to collect the number, or to change the number for the correct one. If you are showing more than one dog, you will most probably have both or all of your numbers attached to your ring clip, and the error is just that you have the wrong number showing, which you can correct immediately yourself.

If the benches are miles away – which they are sure to appear in such circumstances – and you don't have a helpful friend who is willing to sprint a marathon, you could write the correct number boldly on a card, perhaps one that another exhibitor has finished with. This is by no means ideal, but in extreme circumstances it will suffice for, after all, you will technically be wearing your correct number for the judge to see.

On the subject of ring numbers, if you have a coated breed, do try to avoid getting your dog's coat tangled up in your ring clip. This can cause him discomfort, apart from playing havoc with the coat when you want it to look its very best.

Waiting in the wrong class

Granted you probably feel very stupid if you go into the ring in the incorrect class. By this I mean that you have entered the right one, but have somehow gone into a class too soon, or even too late, which is worse because that means you have missed your class. Always keep a very careful eye on the judging before you are due to go in the ring yourself, for judging can speed up almost imperceptibly if there is a high absentee rate in one particular class or if, as is often the case in Maiden and Novice classes, many of the exhibits have already been seen by the judge in a previous class, making the judging of that class very much quicker.

If you have been unfortunate enough to miss your class, ask the steward what you should do. KC rules can change so it would be unwise of me to spell out categorically what is likely to happen, just in case of future alterations to the rules. In any event, if you have missed your class you will have missed your chance of entering in the most appropriate one, so keep your wits about you and make sure you and your dog are in the right place at the right time.

Dropping something

Exhibitors frequently seem to drop things in the ring, most usually a brush, comb or ring number. If this happens when you are moving your dog, it is best to ignore it temporarily for you do not want to put your dog out of his stride, nor to distract the judge and waste time by picking it up there and then. Very often an observant ring steward will see what has happened and will pick it up for you at a discreet moment and will pass it to you when you get back to your place in the line of dogs at the edge of the ring. However, you may not be so fortunate, so just complete your individual assessment as normal and discreetly pick up your dropped item on the way back to your place or, if you are not passing it easily, wait until an appropriate moment to collect it without getting in anyone's way.

Left your comb on the table?

Especially if you have a small, long-coated breed, on the table you are likely to put final touches to your dog's coat whilst the previous exhibitor is moving. As time goes on it will be second nature to pick up your comb or brush as you are about to move around the ring yourself, but when you first start showing you might just forget. This can very easily happen if you are showing a Yorkshire Terrier when you have to deliberately place your brush on the table in order that the judge can use it to more precisely determine coat colour.

So, if you do happen to leave something on the table, the chances are that by the time you have finished moving your dog it will have been moved onto the table at which the judge and stewards sit; otherwise it would be in the way of the next dog to be assessed. When you get back to your place therefore, just go discreetly up to the stewards' table, ideally behind other exhibitors if space allows, and ask to collect your brush or comb.

Your dog misbehaves

Hopefully you have had plenty of practice before attending the first show at which your dog is to compete because it is important that you are in full control of your dog at the show, both inside and outside the ring.

There are many different ways in which a dog might misbehave, and many different reasons why he does so. Most people will excuse an exuberant puppy, in fact it can be great fun watching a puppy's antics in the ring, whilst his owner is literally smothered in

Here the author is inspecting the teeth and bite of a Russian Black Terrier, so it is important to train your dog to allow this to be done without reluctance on the dog's part.

embarrassment as she fails to control his wily ways. Puppies can do all sorts of things to get attention, and even experienced showgoers can occasionally get caught out in this way. Obviously if this happens you should never be rough or harsh with your dog, just show firm control so that he understands exactly who is boss.

An aggressive dog is another matter entirely, and if your dog shows aggression in any way you should immediately ask permission to withdraw it from the ring. If you do not do so you can rest assured that it will be sent out in any case and its misdemeanour reported to the Show Secretary from where the complaint will go to the KC. Aggression in the showring is not to be tolerated, nor indeed is aggression outside the ring. Exhibitors must bear in mind that there are often several thousands of dogs at a show and that an aggressive dog can cause chaos to ensue.

Your dog should not be aggressive toward other dogs or to people. Obviously dogs will 'spark off' at each other from time to time, and in some breeds, such as in many Terriers, this is accepted and almost encouraged by exhibitors so that the dog stands on its toes and is fully alert. However, people who allow their dogs to do this have their dogs completely under control, and in any case it is frowned on by many, especially people not involved with those breeds in which it is commonplace. The most important thing is that you as an exhibitor never allow your dog to come into contact with another dog so that a fight may be set off.

If your dog attacks a judge, this is very serious business. Some dogs can suddenly fly at a judge without warning and without the judge having harmed them in any way. If your own dog has any tendency toward this behaviour the showring is not the place for him, for both you and your dog will land in serious trouble.

Your dog doesn't show well

As a novice exhibitor with a novice dog, you will both have a lot to learn in the months and years ahead, so don't get too uptight if your dog doesn't perform as well as you would wish at first. Time is young yet, for both of you, and you both still have a lot to learn. Always remember that even the most experienced exhibitors sometimes have difficulty getting their young stock to perform well in the ring, so you are not alone.

If your dog doesn't stand well at any point when the judge is looking at him, don't lose your temper. That would be the very worst thing to do! It may be nerves or over-enthusiasm that is making him behave badly. Try to remain calm and be firm but confident with him. Every dog has to get used to new situations and environments. It may be that he needs to gain more experience under male judges, or even female ones; often a dog seems to have a preference. If this is the case, say he doesn't seem to like male judges, get your male friends to go over him at home so that he can see they will not harm him. Soon he will begin to learn that there is nothing to fear in the showring either.

It may be that he objects to having his teeth looked at by a judge. This can often be because he is going through a change of mouth, from puppy to adult teeth, and his reluctance should soon pass when his gums are less sore. Most judges will be gentle with puppies' mouths and of course if you prefer you can show the mouth yourself, in fact if he is showing distress when the judge tries to look inside, he may ask you to show it as a matter of course.

Fear is a great and difficult problem to counteract in a dog, so you will have to empower him with all your confidence and support. This is no time for you to lack confidence personally, for as I have said before this will travel straight down the lead. Neither should you mollycoddle your canine friend. You must certainly give him praise if he performs well, but don't pander to him too much when he expresses fear.

As your puppy grows up there may be other things that will set him back a little in the showring, just as you begin to think you have got things all sorted out. If you have a dog, he may be sensitive around his back end whilst his testicles are developing so you will have to be in total control of him whilst the judge is going over him so that he doesn't turn around and, worse still, warn him off. And when your young dog begins to get the idea about ladies he may decide to move around the ring with his nose to the ground looking for the scent of bitches. If your breed is being judged first in the ring on the first day of a Championship Show, it will probably be less of a problem as there will be fewer smells because dogs are always judged before bitches, but on subsequent days there will have been bitches in that same ring beforehand. I personally don't hold with in-season bitches being exhibited at shows, but many people do take their bitches along in season and a dog is certain to pick up their scent. At Open Shows where dogs and bitches are being shown together, often in the same class, the problem of enticing smells is almost certain to be there, but hopefully your dog will take all this in his stride as he gets a bit older.

On the subject of scents in the ring, and this is something that can affect any dog or bitch at any age, frequently dog shows are held on ground where domestic cattle, sheep, goats and even pigs have been shown and these can undoubtedly leave an odour which can be very tempting for a dog. In such circumstances, all you can do is your best and, if necessary, use a small tasty treat to take his mind off those lovely smells which seem to linger particularly well in the grass.

Bitches that are growing up have their own problems, for many can go a little 'scatty' when they are approaching a season, especially their first one. Because you will not know exactly when the first season is due (as a general rule it can be as early as six months or as late as fifteen months depending on the breed, but there can often be exceptions either way), you will not be able to gauge this as well as you can from the second season onward. During a season and for a couple of weeks or so either side, a bitch can be very temperamental due to hormonal changes and this will very probably make her more difficult to handle in the ring. And just as a word of warning, at these times many owners find their bitches can be a little snappy with other bitches, so bear this in mind if you are planning to crate bitches together at a show.

Undescended testicles in a young male

Hopefully both your puppy dog's testicles will have fully descended by the time he is old enough to enter the showring at six months. Sometimes, however, they can be a bit slow, added to which the excitement of the show can cause a dog to retract one or sometimes both, even though when at home or even outside the ring they are clearly evident. The memories of a dear Afghan of mine, now long since gone, come flooding back into my mind for when I entered the ring he regularly managed to withdraw a testicle until the age of about ten months. To counter this I used to hang onto them discreetly under his coat to keep them warm, so that they were both descended by the time the judge went over him. This might well be worth a try if you have the same problem with your young dog.

Of course both testicles must be there in order to have any measure of success in this way, so if you are in any doubt as to whether or not they are fully descended, you should visit your vet for his opinion.

Your dog decides to go to the toilet in the centre of the ring

Hopefully you will have exercised your dog and given him every opportunity to relieve himself well before entering the ring but accidents can still happen occasionally. That same Afghan puppy of mine frequently embarrassed me dreadfully. Knowing his little habit I was always sure to give him plenty of opportunity to go to the loo beforehand, which he did, but still just as we would set off on our triangle for individual movement assessment he would twizzle round on his lead and do just a little more. Not worth doing actually; I think he was just making a statement, or perhaps it was the excitement of it all! Thankfully he grew out of this habit as time progressed.

If you are unfortunate enough for your dog to go to the toilet in the ring, be it a 'pee' or a 'poo', it is your responsibility to clear it away, not that of the steward. Actually many stewards are most helpful and will assist, or at least they may bring the bucket or mop for you if necessary, but they are absolutely not obliged to do so, so please don't depend on them.

As a safety precaution I always carry a small plastic bag in my pocket, so that if ever I were to have the misfortune of a mishap in the ring, I could clear it up immediately, tie up the bag and deposit it in a bin within seconds. More frequently a dog will decide to urinate in the ring which, although it shouldn't happen, isn't such a problem at an outdoor venue on grass. However, in an indoor venue it can be a real nuisance as it means the mop and bucket has to come out before the next dog can move, so do please try to exercise your dog fully beforehand.

Whilst on this rather unpleasant subject, I should perhaps mention what is acceptable if you have a long-coated breed that manages to soil its coat in the ring. This is clearly a real nuisance but under the circumstances, if time permits, it is generally acceptable for you to remove the dog from the class for a moment or two whilst you sort things out. But of course hopefully this will never happen!

Your dog slips its lead

It is essential that you choose the right lead on which to show your dog, but most dogs are shown on a slip lead for the purposes of exhibition, though they should wear a sturdier collar and lead at all other times. However, a slip lead can do exactly what its name implies, slip! Or, more to the point, the dog can slip out of it. It is therefore very important that you have chosen the lead that suits your dog best and that you control your dog carefully so that this can never happen, for if it does it can lead to disaster.

Some suitable leads, especially for the smaller breeds, have an adjustment that can be made so that the lead, though not tight, can fit snugly round the neck. This type of lead is more difficult to slip as it would have to loosen quite a lot to find its way over the skull and ears. Nonetheless, it can happen so you must still take care.

It is essential that you never let go of your dog's lead in the show ring as major problems can ensue if dogs escape or are allowed to get out of control. Here what could have been a dangerous situation has been nipped in the bud by experienced handlers coming to the rescue.

Other leads are much easier for a dog to slip out of, especially if they back off, and hence effectively back out of the lead. This can happen all too easily if a dog is frightened, so you really must exercise extreme care.

It is not at all unknown for a dog to slip its lead in the show ring, not always through fear, and just occasionally the dog will carry on walking alongside its owner as if it were still attached. Whist this is much to be commended, it is not usually the case. Instead a dog on the loose has a tendency to rush away in an endeavour to leave the ring, which can be very dangerous. Usually there are plenty of people around the ring to prevent the dog escaping, but on occasion a dog will get away from its own breed ring and run into another which, apart from the chaos it causes, could have disastrous consequences if it were a small dog rushing into a ring full of larger dogs and taking them by surprise.

Bearing all this in mind, please make every endeavour to keep your dog on its lead at all times, both inside the ring and out.

Falling over in the ring

When showing your dog it is very important that you, the exhibitor, keep your footing, though unfortunately accidents can, and do, sometimes happen. In an ideal world, outdoor rings would be as flat as bowling greens, but sadly they are not. Occasionally the grass is not quite as short as we would like and very often there are dips in the ground. In rainy conditions when judging has to be under cover, on grass in a tented area, there can be some very awkward muddy patches which can easily cause dogs and exhibitors to slip. Indoor venues often have quite slippy floors so if you are not moving on the rubber matting you might also just slip, especially as you negotiate a bend.

Of course if you fall in the ring it is only natural for you to feel a little foolish, but I can assure you that the ringside audience will be most concerned about whether or not you have hurt yourself. But your main concern will probably be your dog, so do try to hang on to the lead at all costs!

Your dog is taken ill at a show

Hopefully this will never happen, but if your dog is taken ill at a show you will be glad to know that veterinary assistance will always be at hand for this is one of the responsibilities of the show management. At small shows and canine events a vet will rarely be present, but a local practitioner will certainly have been alerted to be on call in case of an emergency. Large Championship Shows have a vet on site and somewhere around the showring, usually near the Secretary's tent, you will find a notice saying 'Vet'. This is where the vet will be stationed if he is not off on call for another emergency somewhere on the showground.

So if you have an urgent problem with your dog, such as a cut on the pad, a sprain, heat exhaustion or any other unforeseen illness such as sudden lethargy, take yourself over to the veterinary tent straight away, though you will of course be expected to pay for any treatment your dog receives.

CHAPTER 9

HAVE YOU WON OR LOST?

Getting to the show and taking your dog into the ring are precursors for what you really want to do, which is to win. Sadly you will not always be at the front of the line of winners and maybe your dog won't be placed at all, but you will have to learn to accept your losses with good grace, hoping that you will have more success on the next occasion.

Placing dogs at the end of a class

In every class, when the judge has assessed each dog individually and has stood back to take that final look, he will select his class winners. There are usually five places in each class, but at small shows there may only be four, whereas in exceptional cases, such as the Open classes at Crufts there are seven.

These places are not all called by their position, but are First, Second, Third, Reserve, Very Highly Commend, Highly Commend and Commend. There will always be a prize card awarded for each place, and at smaller shows probably rosettes too, though maybe only for first place. At breed shows it is more likely that rosettes will be given at least down to third place and possibly beyond. In Britain the usual colour for a first prize is red, whilst a second is blue, but overseas a first prize award is generally blue.

Just occasionally a judge withholds one or more awards through lack of merit. Clearly this is disappointing for the owners of the dogs concerned, but the judge's decision is final and you have elected to seek his opinion. If he really doesn't like your dog, you will know not to enter under him again with the same one.

So, you are standing in the line at the moment the judge is about to make his decisions and hopefully you will have your dog looking his very best, but you will also be keeping a careful eye on the judge to see whether or not he is looking at you to call you into the centre of the ring. If you are in a small class comprising just a handful of dogs, it is likely that the judge will place the dogs straight away as he intends them to be, but he is well within his rights to change them over at the very last moment if he wishes, so if you find yourself standing at the front of the line don't congratulate yourself too heartily until the judge has given the steward the nod and the winners' numbers are called out for the ringside to hear.

In a larger class, although the judge may place the dogs immediately he may also decide to call out a few dogs for his shortlist. If there are five places in the class he may just pull out five for further consideration, but he may select as many as he wishes at this stage so there may be more, some of which will eventually be unplaced. If the judge has done this, he will probably ask you all to move back into a line and then to move again, either collectively in a circle round the ring, or individually. From this final cut he will then make his placings, though remember that he is still at liberty to alter the places around until the very last moment.

If yours is a dog that has been seen in a previous class the judge should have given it another brief look after he has seen all his new dogs. Should there be more than one seen dog in the class they will have been positioned in an order according to prior placings. Then, if the judge so chooses, these dogs will be slotted in amongst the other prize winners. It is indeed conceivably possible that a dog from an earlier class wins ahead of all the others, which is very gratifying for the owner.

Generally a judge will not reverse the position of his seen dogs, but there are occasions when this can happen, and with good cause. If, for example, two dogs were placed first and second in one of the lower classes, and then competed together again in a higher class without meeting any additional competitors, it is normal that they will stay in that order. If however, the judge decides to move them again and the one that stood ahead of the other completely goes to pieces on the move, the judge would be well within his rights to reverse the positions if he saw fit.

In Britain a judge must always place dogs from his left to right, starting with the first prize winner. In other countries it is quite different, dogs most often being pulled out in reverse and therefore building up to a climax when the first prize winner is selected. This can cause some confusion for judges when visiting the UK from overseas, but the rule is that one must judge according to the rules of the host country and to the Kennel Club Breed Standards as issued by that country. So if you are fortunate enough to be placed, make sure you follow instructions clearly as to where and in which position the judge wants you to stand.

Having announced his major winners at this Championship event, judge, Jeff Horswell, extends a congratulatory handshake.

In dog showing it is important to be a good sport, so it is general practise for the second and usually also the third prize winner to congratulate the person standing at the top of the line. Now will not be the time to get into deep conversation but a quick 'Well done!' will suffice.

The winners lower down the line will then be asked to leave the ring whilst the judge takes notes on the top winners. How many dogs he takes notes on will depend on the show, at General Open Shows it will be just first, and at Breed or General Championship Shows either two or three. The judge may ask these winners to stay exactly where they are whilst his writes his notes or dictates them into a machine, or he may ask them to stand again in front of the judges' table where he will sit down to make his notes. During this procedure the stewards will be calling the next class into the ring, so make sure you vacate the scene as soon as the judge has finished writing about your dog. Just a very quick 'Thank you' to the judge will be appreciated, but he will certainly not want you to get into deep conversation or to ask questions about what he thought of your exhibit.

Freda Marshall, having placed her class winners, makes notes in her judging book.

If by chance you were one of the prize winners on whom notes were taken and you have a different dog scheduled to be in the very next class, briefly explain this to the steward so that he will give you a moment to collect your next dog. Leave it to the steward to mention this to the judge if necessary. With luck you and your next dog will be back and standing in line by the time the judge commences the next class.

At the end of the judging of your breed the first prize winners will be called in to compete against each other, unless they have been beaten in another class. If for example your dog won first in the Puppy Dog class but was placed second in Novice, he will not be eligible to compete for Best of Sex. If, however, the dog that beat him was not a puppy, your dog will still be eligible to compete for the Best Puppy award.

From the same successful Irish Water Spaniel kennel, this adult and puppy were both placed in their respective Gundog and Gundog Puppy Groups at a Championship Show.

Once again, the type of show and the classes that were on offer will determine the final challenges. If there were separate classes for dogs and for bitches, for example at a Championship Show, the Best Dog and Reserve Best Dog will usually be selected before the bitch judging commences. Most judges will also declare a Best Dog Puppy winner at this stage, but this must be done after the adult awards have been made. In separate sex judging the same procedure will take place after the bitch judging and then Best Dog and Best Bitch will compete against each other and one will be awarded Best of Breed. The Best of Breed winner will later compete against all other breed winners within its Group or, if the show is not held on the Group system, will be directly in contest for Best in Show.

At Championship Shows in breeds for which Challenge Certificates are on offer, the Judge will most probably also award a CC and Reserve CC to what he considers to be the best exhibits in each sex, but as mentioned earlier, he is at liberty to withhold these if he does not believe the Best of Sex and Reserve Best of Sex winners to be of sufficiently high quality. He must, however, always award a Best of Sex (and Reserve Best of Sex if available) and a Best of Breed.

The Hound Group winner's owner literally jumps for joy as the judge announces that it is his dog that has won Best in Show.

Now cool, calm and collected again, both dog and owner stand for the press photo with judge, Miss Jean Lanning JP.

It is also worth noting that when awarding the CCs, the Reserve CC need not necessarily go to one of the first prize winners. Frequently a judge will call back into the ring the dog that stood second in its class behind the CC winner. Even so, he may still, in the end, decide to give the award to another dog, but it would be perfectly in order if he chose to give it to the second placed dog.

After Best of Breed has been declared the winning puppies will challenge for Best Puppy in Breed and at Open Shows, or at the few Championships where it is on offer, will then compete for Best Puppy in Group and Best Puppy in Show. At single breed club shows the Best of Breed automatically becomes the Best in Show winner, but the Best Opposite Sex may not necessarily be Reserve Best in Show if the judge decides to call in the Reserve Best of Sex who stood behind the Best in Show winner, in which case Best in Show and Reserve may possibly be of the same sex.

As you can see, the competition at the end of the show can be rather confusing for the newcomer, but if you have been lucky enough to win, just keep your eyes and ears open so that if you are called into the ring to challenge you and your dog are there ready and waiting.

Winning trophies

At many breed club shows following the Best in Show and Best Puppy in Show competition there are other challenges, such as for Best Junior, Best Post Graduate and so on. This is because many people will have donated trophies to the society over the years and these will be decided upon and awarded at the show. If you are fortunate enough to

The heavily laden trophy table at the Welsh Corgi show.

win a trophy with your dog you will almost certainly be asked to sign for it if you wish to take it home with you, but you can leave it in the safe-keeping of the club if you prefer. Usually, though, trophies may only be taken home by members of the society holding the show. The fact that you cannot take the trophy home with you does not in any way detract from your win, but allocation to members only gives the organisers a more reliable way of tracing the trophy should it go missing, or not be returned at the next show. Most trophies are held for a period of one year only, but occasionally a small 'token' trophy is given outright.

Although competed for by many different breeds with their roots in various corners of the world, it was this Welsh Terrier that won the Welsh Top Puppy competition.

Trophies come in all shapes and sizes and some of them are truly magnificent with lots of history behind them. It is probably unfair to single out any one club, but one that stands out in my own mind is the Deerhound Club with which I am familiar as the Deerhound is one of my own breeds. The table at the Breed Club's annual event is always absolutely heaving, with stunningly crafted pieces of artwork and several trophies made of sterling silver. What a thrill it is to win one of these wonderful pieces and to have it grace one's home for a year, perhaps sometimes pondering on whose hands it has been in over the many decades during which it has been awarded. But as a trophy winner, however great or small that trophy may be, you have a duty to keep it in good order and to return it either on or before the following year's show.

When and when not to wear rosettes and badges

It is lovely to win a rosette and of course you may wear this as you walk around the show after judging if you wish. However, if you are in a subsequent class or are fortunate enough to have won a first prize and therefore compete later in the challenge you cannot wear your rosette in the ring. If you decide to keep your rosette in your pocket whilst you are in the ring, be certain that it does not stick out of your pocket and show, or people will say you are deliberately trying to display it discreetly to signify that you have won previously!

Sometimes winners are presented with sashes and even embroidered jackets. This puppy Whippet is proudly wearing its jacket signifying a recent win.

Of course rosettes are not always on offer at shows, but at some of the larger shows you can actually purchase a rosette to commemorate your win if you really want a rosette as a souvenir. Many exhibitors like to display their rosettes on a wall at home, and certainly some of them are especially lovely and well deserve prominence around your home. If you have been one of the major winners at a breed club show you may even have won a sash, as can often happen at a show abroad. The display of your dog's awards will certainly make a good talking point for family, friends and visitors to the home.

It is usually acceptable to wear badges in the ring, but not if they advertise a

Both Great Dane and owner are clearly delighted by their big win.

canine food product and therefore indicate that you are sponsored by a particular company. Also it is not acceptable for members of the Kennel Club to wear their club badges in the ring. The reason the wearing of certain badges is not allowed is that, although most judges are completely above board when making their decisions, it could be thought that if someone sporting such a badge won a prize, they were being favoured because of their sponsorship or club membership. It is very important that all decisions are seen to be fair.

Taking your wins and losses with good grace

With luck you will have had a good day in your judging ring and will have come away with a prize of some sort so you will probably be in a happy frame of mind. Don't boast about your wins, but doubtless people will ask you if you if you've had a successful day or perhaps congratulate you if they know you've won. In return it is always appreciated if you ask them if their day has been good. If it has, they will doubtless want to share with you their success but, if not, they will probably gloss over the question and pass quickly onto another subject.

A lovely Best in Show win for the Deerhound, Ch. Hyndsight Au Fait, made all the more special by the wonderful trophy presented by Blackpool Championship Show.

On the other hand, if you have been 'thrown out' without having won a prize at all, take it in your stride and consider it a learning experience. Privately you probably didn't really agree with the judge's decisions, but until you have more experience in the dog-showing world yourself you are not really in a position to know why he reached the decisions he did, so don't complain publicly. Just remember that whether you have won or lost, as the saying goes, 'you are taking the best dog home'.

Things to Think About

Remember to congratulate any winners at the head of the line.

If I win a trophy, am I a society member?

Am I wearing any badges that I shouldn't?

Remember not to wear a rosette if I am in another class.

If I win a trophy I must keep it in good order.

And I must remember to return the trophy for the next show.

CHAPTER 10

BREED JUDGING IS COMPLETE

Hopefully whether you have had a successful day with your dog or not, you will remain around the ring to watch the end of breed judging. Whether or not you agree with the judge's decisions, you can learn a great deal by doing so, and you are sure to meet people within the breed with whom you can chat.

At Championship Shows, an award board will be available for all to see, usually positioned in the corner of each ring. So if you have not marked down the class winners in your catalogue as the day has progressed, you will have an opportunity to do this at the end of judging. At Open and Limited Shows, the awards are usually posted on a wall in the venue but of course there will be far fewer dogs in each class at such shows, so it will have been easier to take careful note of the placings from the ringside.

Once breed judging is over, and possibly also during the lunch break if your judge has elected to break for lunch and your own dog has finished being shown, you will have a chance to look round the rest of the show.

Around the trade stands

At Limited and Open Shows and at breed club shows there will most probably only be a couple of trade stands, or maybe a small handful, but at major Championship Shows you will be spoiled for choice. At most shows the stands are located around the perimeter of the show, so you will probably walk a very good distance if you plan to see them all. Sometimes they are located in a separate area of the show ground, which is probably more convenient for the ardent shopper, but unless you make a point of going to that specific area, you may not get to look at any stands at all – so much depends upon the layout of the show.

At first you will probably be overwhelmed by all the stands and the many things they have on offer, but as time goes on you will get to know the ones with which you begin to do regular business, such as where you buy your shampoos, conditioners and extra grooming items. Soon enough the stallholders will get to know your face too, and then you will truly feel like a regular show-goer!

Don't be tempted to buy at the first stall you come to that is selling something that you need or like, for some products vary quite considerably in price from one trade stand to another. Be careful though; not every product is of the very same quality so you will have to weigh up the pros and cons.

This stall is selling all sorts of treats for exhibitors' canine friends. (CUNLIFFE)

As I have mentioned before, you will find many of the trade stand holders extremely helpful for they have been selling the same type of products for many years. Many of them own their own stalls, so have a vested interest in knowing exactly what their clients need for their particular breed of dog.

As you become more and more involved in the show world and more in tune with your dog's needs, you will very probably want to make a few new purchases to add to your grooming equipment. You have probably purchased one of the cheaper hairdryers for starters, but now realise that something rather more substantial would give you better service and speed up your grooming procedure. This will be especially important if you have a long-coated breed and plan to increase the number of dogs you plan to show.

Indeed there are many large and expensive grooming aids that you may aspire to in years to come, such as specially made baths and velocity blasters to blow out the water from the coat. Many different things such as these are used by professional groomers, but increasingly by enthusiastic showgoers also. You will probably spend hours investigating the stalls at shows, especially during the early stages of your show career, and you will fully understand why many exhibitors attend the biggest show of them all, Crufts, on two days, one with their dogs and another to look around the trade stands and make their purchases.

These soft sided dog crates are very useful for well behaved dogs, but the larger size is still heavy and rather cumbersome to carry, especially when not folded. (CUNLIFFE)

But you must never overlook the basics and you will soon discover which are the most essential elements of your grooming box for your particular breed. An interesting recent report provided a good cross-section of items that exhibitors of disparate breeds found the most useful. Of those interviewed, for Irish Setters the one most important item was a pin brush, replaced at roughly three monthly intervals once the pins begin to be displaced; in Keeshonds an exhibitor laid great store on the use of something that is technically a face cleaning product, designed to remove staining from around the eyes. However, it could be put to many other good uses including the removal of urine staining and cleaning up the back end after a loose motion. Olive oil was also considered a very handy item, especially for use on rough, dry noses and cracked pads. Moving on to Irish Water Spaniels a wide toothed metal comb was considered the most important item. This could be used for regular grooming and did not pull out excessive coat, nor did it destroy the curls which are so characteristic of the breed.

One of the breeds with a particularly challenging coat is the Old English Sheepdog, for which an owner swore by high quality brushes made of a combination of boar bristle and nylon, attached to a rubber pad. Three sizes were used and the reason for the bristle content was that it effectively cleans the dog's coat without breaking it. Then, at the smaller end of the scale is the King Charles Spaniel, for which facial scissors were considered essential. These are curved scissors that are rounded at the ends and therefore much safer than conventional scissors for use in delicate areas. They are used to trim facial whiskers, as well as for cutting out excess hair between the pads. In fact for virtually every breed a good quality pair of scissors, or maybe several, is essential and this is brought home by the very fact that one particular company, well-known for scissors, boasts a choice of over 120 different pairs.

Feeding products available at shows

There must be few experienced breeders and exhibitors, however, who would disagree with the fact that good coat quality is actually produced from inside. Yes, the coat can be enormously improved by the use of the right grooming equipment, but the quality must be there in the first place. A high quality diet is incredibly important to the development of all aspects of the dog, including of course its health.

At every big show you will find various manufacturers of canine food products, many of them with a whole team of people working behind the scenes in laboratories to make regular improvements to the food they offer for the betterment of our canine friends. The dog food market is a giant affair and you will undoubtedly be spoiled for choice.

Several of the pet food companies have samples on display, but it is not unknown for the occasional mischievous puppy such as this Grand Basset Griffon Vendeén to help itself, without invitation.

When you bought your first dog you will have received a diet sheet and details of the food on which the puppy was raised. Obviously you should not change the product immediately and you may indeed elect to stay with the same one for the rest of your dog's life, but it is only natural to look around from time to time to see if you feel anything would suit better. I should mention though, that any change must be made gradually. You should never change from one make of food to another simply overnight or your dog will be almost certain to get an upset tummy.

The various food products on offer vary both in price and in quality, and of course in their make up. Some are better suited to one breed than another, and perhaps even to an individual dog. Each manufacturer usually has a wide range on offer, covering feeding requirements through the various stages of a dog's life from tiny puppies to veterans. These will vary in content, with the protein factor being something to consider very seriously, for an active dog will require a much higher protein content than a dog that lives a more sedentary life. There will also be a difference in the size of the kibble, a large breed requiring and being able to cope with bigger chunks of food, whilst a Toy breed will need a small size. Indeed owners of breeds such as Pomeranians, often feed food designed for puppies throughout their dogs' lives, for the kibble is small enough for their tiny mouths and being such an active breed they can generally cope with a reasonably high protein content.

Of course there are tinned foods too, and normal biscuit meal to mix in with that. The varieties and various permutations are virtually endless. You will also have a wide variety of tastes to choose from and at some tradestands, samples are available for your dog to try.

So by going around the canine food stalls at shows, you will certainly be able to see what is available and what type of food is likely to suit your dog best. You will also generally find much more favourable prices at shows than you will in pet stores and large retail outlets. If you have only one dog you may decide to make your food purchases at the show, but if you have more dogs, or perhaps a large breed when a substantial quantity is needed, you may prefer to have the food delivered to your home. All this can be organised at a show and the staff on the various stands will help you every step of the way.

Supplements

Other trade outlets at shows sell various supplements designed to help your dog in so many ways. There are tablets and powders, oils and other liquids, some of which help to

A St Bernard waiting patiently whilst its owner takes advice on which herbal treatments are available. (CUNLIFFE)

develop healthy bone growth in large breeds, others feed the coat from the inside out or perhaps help a bitch to whelp easily, whilst still others counter a nervous disposition, or just give that show dog a little extra spark on the day. Basically if you have a problem with your dog and you want to find something to help improve it you can be certain that at most large shows you will find a trade stand holder who can help you.

Homoeopathic and alternative remedies are now used widely in the dog world and if you look around the bookstalls you will very probably find information that will guide you in the right direction, for homoeopathic remedies are often used to treat different ailments in dogs than in humans.

Buying collectables, gifts and miscellanea

The range of stalls you will find at a large show can be so disparate that it would be difficult to describe them all and at Crufts the variety is even more enormous, in fact one wonders at Crufts if some of the stalls have any direct connection with dogs at all. A dog show is the ideal place to buy some little collectable item for your home, or as a gift for a friend or relative. Quality ranges from the fairly cheap and gaudy to the simply exquisite, so whatever the price bracket you have set yourself you will probably find what you want.

If artwork interests you, you can find prints and original paintings, both old and new. Quite often you will even be able to organise having your dog painted, from life or from photographs. Such artists usually have a selection of their work available for you to see so make sure you are satisfied that the artist is sufficiently talented to do justice to your particular breed of dog.

Then there are things like stationery – gift cards, wrapping paper, notepads and personalised notepaper. As I have already said many times, whatever you need that is canine related you will almost certainly be able to find it at one of the larger dog shows.

Bookstalls and publishers

If you are interested in reading about your breed, or dogs in general, you will usually find some bookstalls at major shows and if they don't have the book you are looking for in stock, they can almost certainly order it, provided it is still in print. However, if it is an older book you have set your mind on, you may just find this at one of the antiquarian bookstalls, a few of which also sell other canine related antiques, so you will find plenty to absorb you here.

Then there are the tradestands hosted by the two weekly canine newspapers (*Our Dogs* and *Dog World*). These attend every Championship show and one of them has a particularly good supply of books on offer too, as well as things like records books so that you can keep a careful track of your dog's wins. Both of course sell their newspapers, and sometimes you can find back copies available too. Towards Christmas time you will also be able to obtain highly useful diaries that list the many canine events due to be held during the coming year and both papers always produce an *Annual*, packed with both adverts and editorial content which will provide plenty to keep you occupied over the winter months when the larger shows are a bit thin on the ground.

The stalls of both newspaper publishers will have show schedules on display, as will many of the other trade stand holders. These you are at liberty to pick up and take home, the purpose of which is twofold for it saves you the trouble of applying for a schedule and saves the show society the cost of a stamp when posting one out to you. Do, though, have a quick look through first of all to see if the show, and indeed the judge are of interest to you. It would be a pity for the many racks of schedules to be utterly depleted by the end of the day because they had been collected without due thought by people who really had no intention of entering the show.

The Kennel Club's Stand

Although not present at every show, the Kennel Club's own stand is a very useful one to visit for here you will be able to obtain information about all aspects of showing and will be able to purchase various booklets to give you essential guidance.

Perhaps most important for you will be a copy of your dog's Breed Standard which hopefully you have already read in a breed book that you purchased when you were first enthused by the breed. However, from the KC stand you will be able to purchase all the Breed Standards in compact form. These are packaged not by breed but by the Group, so although you may at this early stage not want to buy them all you should seriously consider purchasing the Standards for your dog's own Group. Another very useful booklet both for the beginner and for the experienced exhibitor is the KC's *Glossary of Canine Terms*, in which you will find an extensive list of canine terminology that is not always easy to understand.

Is it time to have your dog's photo taken professionally?

Maybe you have done a little winning with your dog, or maybe you've already done a lot. Even if your dog hasn't won much at all yet, it's well worth getting a professional photo taken so that you have a good image ready and waiting when the time comes to advertise. Of course if your puppy is still maturing a photo will only be of temporary value for advertising purposes, but it's still nice to keep as a pictorial memory of what he looked like as a youngster.

In these days of digital cameras, everyone seems to think that they have expertise as a photographer, which may perhaps be so, but a good canine photographer is something else. This is someone who, in the main, has years of experience in having photographed dogs so knows exactly how to bring out your dog's best assets from behind the camera lens. All too frequently one sees poor quality photos included in advertisements, for which people have paid good money, and it is sad they don't realise that their money has not been well spent.

If you have won at a show, you may like to place your advertisement in the canine press there and then. Just go to either the *Our Dogs* or *Dog World* stand and you will be given all the help you need with regard to prices, size and timing. The trade stand manager will even be able to arrange for you to have your dog's photo taken on the showground if you wish.

At virtually any time of the year, from late spring onward, you can place your advertisement for the following year's *Annual*. Both newspapers operate a system by which the earlier you book, the greater discount you will receive, so this is well worth bearing in mind. Also consider that both the weekly newspapers and the *Annuals* are read all over the world, so by advertising you will be bringing your dog's picture and his successes into living rooms across the globe.

A Pembrokeshire Welsh Corgi and its delighted owner pose together for a photo after this memorable win. It is always good to have photos to look back on in years to come.

There can also be occasions on which you choose to advertise in a monthly publication, such as the *Kennel Gazette* or *Dogs Monthly*, both of which produce some issues in which specific breeds are featured. However, you will rarely be able to organise these adverts at shows, but will need to make telephone contact with the publication concerned.

Other countries of course have different canine publications and you will appreciate that it would not be possible to detail them all. Perhaps when you have been showing for a few years and have done a considerable amount of winning you will even consider advertising abroad!

Another method of advertising is in a breed club newsletter or year book. In relation to the size of advert you will receive, this is usually less expensive than an advertisement in the general press, but by no means always so. You should also consider that the readership will be much more selective. Far fewer copies will be printed but the entire readership will be interested in or involved especially with your own breed, which is a great bonus. Most breed club secretaries and year book editors are show goers, so if you don't know who they are yet, ask if someone can introduce you so that you can find out more. Another very important factor in advertising in a club year book is that in doing so you will be helping to promote the club and maybe even to swell the funds a little so that it can better serve its members in the year ahead.

Making time to watch other dogs being judged

Hopefully you will have watched a good deal of the judging around your own breed ring and will have picked up plenty of tips for future shows. But if you can find a while to watch some of the other judging around the show you will learn even more. Take yourself along to the main rings where the stakes classes are judged, although of course the timing of these may not work out well. Generally a guide to what is being judged and in which rings can be ascertained from the paperwork you received with your passes. To watch the Champion Stakes class is always a good exercise for, as its name implies, all the contestants are champions, so you will have the opportunity to see many high quality dogs of various breeds being judged together. Watch carefully how they are being handled and see if you can pick up any ideas that may help you with the presentation of your own breed.

If your own dog is still a puppy or junior, you may like to watch the Puppy Stakes or Junior Stakes classes being judged, in which case see if you can pick up any tips as many of the exhibitors in this class too are highly experienced, some of them professional handlers. And at the other end of the age scale is the Veteran and this is always good to watch so that you can see in what wonderful condition older dogs can be kept if they are looked after properly. This will give you something to aim for in the years ahead.

The final competition of each day in the main ring is Group judging and, on the last day the seven Group winners meet up to determine Best in Show. Following this there may be competition for Best Puppy, but not always. If you get the chance, Group and Best in Show judging is really something you should watch as frequently as you can for it will allow you to see all the day's Best of Breed winners being put through their paces.

Bryn Cadogan is judging the Terrier Group in this large, tented show ring.

It was a wet day outside at this show, but competition for the ultimate Best in Show award was held inside this exquisite marquee. Pictured here are the seven winners of their respective Groups.

You will notice that the breeds within each Group vary considerably. In the Hound Group you have the diminutive scent hound, the Miniature Dachshund, and yet also the largest breed of all, the Irish Wolfhound, which hunts by sight. How, you wonder, can the judge compare these two very different breeds, but of course he is actually judging them against their own Breed Standards. The Utility Group is the most diverse, the breeds in this Group being the ones that don't fit neatly into any other, so you have breeds like the small, long-coated Lhasa Apso and its Sino-Tibetan cousin, the Shih Tzu, competing against a large and powerful breed like the Akita, which hails from Japan.

If you sit by the ringside during Group competition you will learn a very great deal and if you feel you would like to learn more about breeds other than your own you may decide to study their Breed Standards as you watch them. Don't feel embarrassed about this for anyone worth their salt will know that you are doing so to increase your knowledge. It is certainly something I did in my earlier days and although I may have had a few strange glances, I'm glad I did so for I learned a lot this way which has stood me in good stead for judging the many different breeds I do today. Some people of course really have an interest only in their own breed, but I would urge you not to be blinkered and to keep an open mind from the very outset of your participation as an exhibitor.

Making more friends and acquaintances

You will almost undoubtedly have made acquaintances and maybe even friends around your breed ring, especially when you have attended a few shows and have got to know people better. If you are able to spend some time round other rings and around the rest of the showground, you will come into contact with even more people, some of whom you will soon find you get to know by face.

When sitting quietly by another breed ring to watch the judging, you will often find that you get into conversation with your neighbour, who is probably gratified that someone from outside their own breed is taking an interest in it. It can often be quite fun to get into deep conversation with a dyed-in-the-wool Terrier man who knows his breed inside out and is at pains to explain it to you. Oh yes, keep your eyes and ears open and a smile on your face and you'll get to learn a lot!

Things to Think About

What might I need to buy from the trade stands?

Do I need any extra grooming items?

Should I order dog food at the show?

Visit the Kennel Club Stand if at the show.

Shall I have my dog's photo taken yet?

Remember to watch other dogs being judged.

CHAPTER 11

AFTER THE SHOW

Although you probably set out from home at the very crack of dawn, your day at the dog show will seem to have flown by and all too soon you will be ready to wend your way home, with millions of things rushing through your head about the day you have just experienced.

Finding your way to the car

You will remember that I gave you a word of warning about knowing exactly where you parked your car. Now is the time that you will have to put your memory cells into action. Firstly you will have to be sure that you are leaving the showground from the correct exit. At some venues there may only be one exit, but at many there are several. At shows such as those held at Birmingham's National Exhibition Centre there seem like millions, numbered 3.1, 3.2, 3.3 and so on. Also, a showground can often present quite a different appearance at the end of the day from that at the beginning, making it easy to lose your bearings.

Dog show car parks can be large and sometimes congested, so keep your patience and always be sure your dog does not get overheated whilst the car is stationary. (CUNLIFFE)

There can also be the added problem of weather conditions. Perhaps you arrived when it was dry, bright and sunny, but if the day turned out to have heavy downpours the ground underfoot, particularly at an outdoor venue, may have become like a quagmire, making the going difficult, particularly if you are trying to pull a trolley packed not only with dogs but with purchases too. Most show societies will do their very best to keep conditions underfoot as firm as possible, often putting down straw and sometimes special matting, but still the journey homeward can be something of a trial in inclement weather conditions.

In the car park

Assuming that you have found your car relatively easily, or perhaps when you are almost at your wits' end depending on the quality of your memory cells, you will have to pack everything back into the car, which somehow always seems to take longer than it does to get it out!

Take great care not to allow your dog to escape in the car park, though if it is beginning to empty out this might just be a good opportunity to take your dog for a last walk on the lead, always remembering to take with you that all important 'poo' bag. And if you have had to use it, please don't leave it under the car wheel and drive off leaving it behind. If there is no suitable receptacle handy you will just have to take it home with you. The last thing dog enthusiasts need is for venues to be withdrawn for use because of the state in which exhibitors leave the grounds. This happens all too often, even at small breed club events, and it can be enormously difficult to locate a suitable new venue at a realistic price on the required dates. The result is that the organisers are put under additional pressure

Just occasionally car parks can turn into veritable quagmires, but show organisers usually arrange for a tractor to be on hand in case cars or caravans need to be towed out.

and it is often necessary to increase entry fees because of the additional costs involved. And all because of a handful of thoughtless exhibitors!

Should you find yourself in the unfortunate situation of locating your car in a quagmire, don't despair. Although this is a real nuisance, at major shows there is a usually a tractor on hand to pull you off. In fact in really bad conditions it has been known for tractors to have to tow caravans onto the caravan park, as well as off at the close of the show!

The long drive home

Although you have so much to think about at the end of a long and exciting day, never forget that your dog is the reason you went to the show and your dog will be with you in the car all the way home. Remember his comforts. He may need to stretch his legs en route and to have a drink of water if you have not fitted out his travelling compartment with a non-spill bowl. Just as you remembered to take spare water for your dog on the journey to the show, don't forget it when travelling back also.

Be prepared for a queue of traffic getting out of the show's car park. You may drive straight to the exit, but depending on what time you leave there could be a bottle-neck, so don't get impatient at the very start of your journey.

If you have had a good show there will be lots to talk about on the journey home, and if you have no travelling companion you can always spill your heart out to your dog. He won't mind, though doubtless he won't fully understand; his mind will probably be preoccupied with memories of all the magnificent smells his nostrils enjoyed during the day. But however excited you are, do drive carefully and don't run out of petrol!

Arrival home

Remember that your first concern is still your dog. You may have had a long, hard, but enjoyable day yourself, but so has your dog and he must still be foremost in your thoughts, so get him out of the car and safely into your garden to stretch his legs before unpacking the car and making yourself a cup of tea.

I am terribly lazy about unpacking the car fully the evening I have returned from a show, but that is a bad habit to get into and I can assure you it's not much fun finding the odd stale banana floating round in the bottom of your grooming bag a couple of days later. In addition, the schedules you so carefully collected at the show may be past their closing date by the time you unpack your show bag, so try to get yourself into a good routine from the very start of your dog's show career.

Beginning to understand the dog press better

Now that you have been to your first dog show you will have begun to see what all the hype is about. It's a big world out there and for the time being you will be a very small fish in a very large sea. You may have purchased one or both of the weekly canine newspapers at the show, or you may have ordered them from your newsagent, or even from the

This high quality Tibetan Terrier was selected as Best of Breed by the author (RIGHT)*, going on to win the Utility Group and Reserve Best in Show under judge, Ann Arch* (LEFT)*. Denys Simpson* (CENTRE) *is representing the Welsh Kennel Club.*

publishers themselves which is a very efficient way of organising things because there is every chance the paper will arrive through your letter box on Thursday rather than on Friday, the official publication day for each of them. However you obtain them, you will surely be anxious to read all about the show you have visited at the weekend.

The majority of general Championship Shows get good editorial coverage in both papers within a few days of the show, but coverage of Open Shows is far less comprehensive and is frequently very much later, combining the judging critiques with a short review of the show, though not always. If there has been a professional photographer representing one of the canine newspapers at an Open Show, there will usually be at least one editorial photograph of the major winners and, for a relatively small charge, exhibitors will have been offered the opportunity to place a photo-advertisement for their successful exhibits, so together this makes an interesting feature.

All judges are obliged to write a critique on the winners of the classes they have judged and to submit them to the dog press shortly after the show. These critiques then eventually appear in the press for everyone to read and can be interesting not only to the owners of the dogs concerned but also to other dog owners, particularly whose dogs were also judged within the breed at that show. Take a good look at these critiques and see if you can figure out why the judge chose the winners he did, whether or not your own dog was amongst them. It has to be said that the quality of judges' critiques varies considerably, not

The seven Group winners compete for Best in Show.

all judges are adept at writing and in any event notes have to be taken in a very short space of time. Don't therefore take every critique as the gospel truth, for it is not unknown for one judge to praise a dog's correct layback of shoulder and for another to criticise it! You must also bear in mind that every judge's interpretation of the Breed Standard will be slightly different, the various points of the dog viewed in a different way and with more or less emphasis placed upon them. This is another reason why different people's critiques about the same dog can vary somewhat, as can the fact that a particular dog may simply perform better at one show than at the next.

Doubtless you will want to read the breed notes in the weekly canine publication and sooner or later, if you have had a good win with your dog you may just find your name in print there. For most breeds there is one designated regular columnist for each paper, but occasionally there are two, usually if it is thought prudent to give a wider perspective.

Breed notes are a wonderful vehicle to disseminate news. Different correspondents give their own personal style to these columns, and although Championship Show reports are given elsewhere in the paper, the breed note correspondent usually also gives each show a brief mention. Here, too, is the place to find about breed shows, both before and after the event, and news of any members of the specific breed that have had a particularly good win at a Limited or Open Show, or at some Special Event, such as those organised on a geographical basis. It is in this column that you will probably keep abreast of news such as forthcoming breed seminars, rescue matters and even births, illnesses and deaths, the latter both canine and human.

When you have a leisurely moment at home, it is also interesting to look though the breed notes concerning breeds that are not your own for often you can pick up some very useful information. Maybe a veterinary problem is discussed or explained, or perhaps some useful grooming tip or a hint about a natural medicine to help with poor pigmentation or a coat problem. I urge you not to be blinkered, for you will be able to learn a great deal from what is happening in other breeds as well as your own.

This German Shepherd Dog (Alsatian) is being presented to perfection for a photo that will forever be cherished in the photo album.

Sporting her winner's rosettes, this exhibitor is taking time out with her German Pinschers before competition later in the day.

Each of the two canine weekly newspapers has regular columnists writing on a wide range of topics covering all aspects of the dog-showing world. Some of the information is topical, and can provoke much comment in the 'letters columns', whilst other features cover history, art, natural remedies, veterinary topics, obedience, junior handling and so on. Absolutely no aspect of our sport is omitted, so you will always find something of interest to read and the weekly papers will keep you absorbed for many a long hour.

At the back of each paper is the show and commercial advertisement section, and by now you will hopefully already have got used to scanning these pages with a fine toothcomb. Advertisements for forthcoming shows give the date and venue of the show as well as the closing date for entries, so if you don't already have a schedule you will be able to telephone to obtain one in good time. Some of these adverts also list breeds classified and the names of the judges so you can see if there are classes suitable for you before you ring.

Educational events also appear in the dog press, so even if you are relatively new to the world of dogs you may find a seminar that will be of interest to you. These seminars are sometimes breed specific, hosted by breed clubs, and sometimes relate to training for up-coming judges and those who are interested in stewarding.

Thinking about stewarding

Although it will be a good while before you are in a position to get your foot on the first rung of the ladder toward becoming a dog judge, stewarding is a very good way of becoming more involved and getting to know the ropes. All societies need stewards at shows. Usually two are assigned to each judging ring and although one clearly needs to have substantial experience, often the other is relatively new so if this is an aspect that interests you, why not approach a local society or even a breed club to see if you might help in this way? In fact it is a KC rule that those who judge at high level have to have had stewarding experience, so it is worth keeping a careful note of your experience in this field in case it is needed in the future.

Things to Think About

Find the right exit from the show.

Carry fresh water for my dog on the journey home.

Unpack the car fully when I get home.

Make full use of the dog papers.

Do I think I'd enjoy stewarding?

The Deerhound, Modhish Lillie Langtree, handled and owned by Carol Ann Johnson, canine photographer; co-bred by Miss Johnson and the author. (POOLE)

CHAPTER 12

WHERE DO I GO FROM HERE?

Now that you have received your first taste of dog showing you will have some idea whether or not it is a hobby with which you want to be involved for many years to come. The majority of people who begin dog showing don't really stay the course. It is said that a dog show person's average number of years of involvement is only five. That may come as some surprise, particularly bearing in mind all the effort, time and investment they have put into their new hobby over such a short spell, but the reasons for dropping out can be many fold, not least of which is the fact that they realise they are not doing the amount of winning they would like.

So, as we begin to draw to the close of this book, let us now take a look at what you have learned during your early days in the show ring, and what lies ahead.

Am I aiming too high?

You have a show dog that you have exhibited at shows, but you must firstly consider whether your dog has proved to be of sufficiently good quality to exhibit and, if so, at what level. You will already know whether or not your dog has won any prizes in the show ring. If he has that's a very good start, but you must also consider amongst what competition he has won. Has it been in large classes, or just small ones, and has the quality of the competition with him in the class been strong?

Whilst it's lovely to win a red rosette or prize card, if yours was the only exhibit in the class that wasn't really much of a challenge, was it? Yes, the judge could have withheld, but especially if you were exhibiting at Open level or lower, most judges are reluctant to withhold, although really they should if they think a dog's quality insufficiently high. If of course your dog has regularly been placed highly in large classes at Championship Shows, that's quite another matter. You can't realistically expect your dog to be in the cards at every show for every judge's choice is different but if your dog wins a place more often than not in classes where other dogs have been unplaced, then you probably really do have a good potential show dog.

If you haven't been overly successful with your dog at the first few shows you have attended, you will need to ask yourself why. Do you think it is the dog's quality and conformation to the Breed Standard that is lacking, or might it be your own expertise as a handler and the quality of your dog's presentation? These are very serious issues, though each of them can be addressed if you really wish you continue with this interesting hobby.

A successful Junior Handler and a Rottweiler, judged by Patsy Hollings.

But before we begin to consider how best they can be addressed, we should look at what you expect to get out of dog showing.

What are my goals?

Maybe you have decided that the big dog shows are really not for you. The competition is too fierce, people are not as friendly as you hoped they would be and you are probably finding that the financial outlay and time involved is just too high. That may be a fair appraisal of the situation, and if you don't aspire to do any particularly big winning with your dog you can still find enjoyment at shows at a lower level. Open and Limited Shows will cost considerably less to enter and the distance you will have to travel to them will be less too. Added to this, although there will always be a few really high quality dogs at the show, there will be many that are not so good, so you will stand a greater chance of winning the occasional prize card, maybe even lots of them.

Certainly, however good the quality of your dog, you will be able to have lots of fun at Companion Shows, and you are almost certain to pick up the odd prize or two here. Added to which the financial outlay will be even less. The rewards to be gained from all these shows is great, for here you will find plenty of like-minded people, with several of whom you are likely to strike up friendships. Such shows provide an enjoyable day out for you and your dog whether you are travelling to the show alone or with a companion.

Clearly if you have chosen dog showing as a hobby you love dogs, and if you have attended a few shows and now have a wider perspective on the world of dogs you will have realised that there are many avenues of interest out there. Perhaps you have been attracted

If you eventually decide that dog showing is not the sport for you, you may like to take part in Obedience and one day perhaps your dog will take part in a major display, as these perfectly trained Golden Retrievers have done.

There are lots of other ways in which you can enjoy challenges with your canine friend. This dog is taking part in the 'Clever Cavalier' display at Crufts.

to Agility work, Obedience, Flyball or even Heelwork to music, in each of which success is dependent on the ability of your dog, not on its beauty points. Maybe one of these is a route you would like to follow so that you are still involved with the world of dogs, but in a different way, though still highly competitive. Obviously if you go along this avenue, your own training skills will play a very important part in the success or otherwise of your dog. As time progresses the two of you will learn to work in tandem and you may well reap just rewards in another aspect of the dog game. From time to time these various activities are drawn together at a show, such as at Crufts, which provides a marvellous opportunity to observe the many different sports involving dogs, as well as the way dogs can be of enormous benefit to us human beings!

Agility trials are very popular and help to keep both owner and dog fully active.

It may be that thus far you have only attended the smaller shows which, after all, is what I recommended from the outset. If your dog has won fairly consistently at these shows you may now feel ready to move on to bigger shows at which you will meet stiffer competition. But it is all too easy to get a big ego boost at smaller events and then to attend your first few Championship Shows, only to find that your dog is consistently unplaced. This being the case you will have to think again. If you have been truly bitten by the show bug maybe you will have to consider buying another show dog, but that is something we shall come to in a moment.

Do I need to improve my own handling skills?

Now that you have been to shows and have seen the skill and expertise with which some people present and handle their dogs, you will be in a better position to assess your own skills in this regard. If you haven't done as much winning as you think your dog deserves, is it perhaps because you have not presented him to perfection, either by way of his stance or movement in the show ring, or by the manner in which you have presented his coat? These problems are not insurmountable, they just involve more practice.

Take yourself back to ringcraft classes if you have stopped going, or even locate one of the privately run training classes for which you will have to pay a more substantial fee but at which you will obtain more personal tuition. Here there will probably be large mirrors at least on one side of the training venue, so that you can see exactly the picture you are making with your dog. Some people even have a large mirror erected in perhaps the grooming room at home so that they can see exactly what their dog will look like to the judge when being presented in the ring.

If you have a coated breed, maybe you need more help and guidance in presenting your dog so that it truly looks its best. Many breed clubs, especially of the coated breeds, offer occasional seminars to help newcomers learn the ropes. If you have a long-coated breed like a Lhasa Apso, Maltese or Afghan Hound, it is essential that you do not take out too much of the coat when grooming, but on the other hand you must eliminate every

A photo to remember – This Shetland Sheepdog with the shield it has won commemorating all previous winners.

vestige of a possible knot. A Terrier can be ruined visually by incorrect coat preparation, but conversely its beauty can be enhanced dramatically in the hands of someone skilled in the art of trimming. Again, I stress that you should watch other exhibitors carefully, learn as much as you can by observation and don't be afraid to ask questions at the appropriate time. Top handlers will never give away all their secrets, but you are sure to pick up the odd tip or two until you have reached the level of having a few secrets of your own.

Learning more about my breed

If you are to become a truly dedicated breed enthusiast you will want to learn as much as possible about your breed. Only in this way will you be in a position to evaluate the quality of your own dog. Too many people in the dog showing world are kennel blind, simply not seeing, or not admitting to, the faults their dogs have. This is another form of being blinkered and people who are kennel blind are unlikely to progress very far in gaining any measure of real success in the showring.

These dogs are both Spitz breeds, but the Samoyed (LEFT) is a member of the working Group, whilst the diminutive Pomeranian belongs in the Toy Group.

Winning Best in Show at Crufts surely has to be the pinnacle of a dog's show career. This magnificent Australian Shepherd Dog, winning BIS under judge Brenda Banbury in 2006, had travelled over for the show all the way from the USA.

Always check the breed notes and educational events in the dog press so that you don't miss an opportunity of attending a seminar at which you can learn more, perhaps even getting the chance to obtain 'hands on' experience by going over dogs taken along for the purpose. When people realise that you have been in the breed a little while and are anxious to learn more, you may even be invited to go over their own dogs to learn still more about the construction of your breed. An experienced breeder and exhibitor will probably be only too happy to point out to you their own dogs' better points, and if you are lucky they might just point out some of the bad ones too! But in the latter case, if a dog's faults have been mentioned to you in confidence please never discuss them with anyone else. Not only would this be unfair on the person who had tried to share with you their own experience, but if word gets around, which it will, you may never be given the opportunity to go over someone else's dog again.

Another thing I would urge you to do is to watch the higher classes being judged at

Championship and Breed Club Shows. Check discreetly in your catalogue to see which are the champions amongst them, and try to ascertain in your own mind why they have reached this high accolade. Granted, some may have achieved the odd CC as a result of favours being granted or, especially in the numerically small breeds, they may on occasion not have been up against stiff competition, but none have won fewer than three CCs under different judges, and many of them have won even more. Having said that, every judge is entitled to his or her own opinion, and even as a novice exhibitor you are sure to see dogs that you believe to be more typical of their breed than others.

Another question you can ask yourself when watching other dogs being judged is why some dogs seem not to be winning as highly as you feel they should. Is it the handling or presentation? Is it the speed at which they are being moved, or perhaps the dog's ring presence? Perhaps you can learn a lesson from this too?

Dog shows have developed enormously over the last few decades, as has the presentation of dogs. Indeed it is often sad to see some well-respected breeders and exhibitors with beautifully constructed, typical stock, failing to win the highest awards merely because they are a little behind the times in terms of presentation. Be aware of this too, and hopefully when you have more experience yourself you will achieve just the right balance, owning highly typical stock that is presented to perfection.

Should I get another show dog?

By now you will have some idea of what you expect from the show world. The dog you bought for the showring may have turned out well, or perhaps is not as good as you anticipated or hoped for. Whichever way around, the time will probably come when you want to have another show dog. It may be that you recognise the limitations of your first dog, that he is not of sufficient quality to win high awards, so perhaps you will retire him from the show ring, just keeping him as a much-loved pet, or maybe you will restrict his competitive events to those at a lower level. In this case you will probably want to get another dog to show more competitively, with a greater chance of success.

If your dog is already winning well and you have tasted the sweet smell of success, perhaps you will decide that you want another dog to show too, maybe in a class for the opposite sex, or if your dog is now in the adult classes you might like a puppy to bring out. Maybe you have even decided that you would like to breed, so you will already be making plans for the future.

Most people actually buy in their second show dog as well as the first, for two principal reasons. It has to be said that to successfully exhibit a dog that one has bred oneself is more rewarding than winning with a dog bred by someone else, so if you have decided to breed you may have contemplated breeding from your very first show dog. However, there are two very serious aspects to consider. If the bitch you have hasn't been winning particularly well in the showring, she may simply not be of a sufficiently high standard from which to breed. In my opinion, and I hope in the opinion of most dedicated dog people, if a dog is worthy of being bred from it should also be worthy of competing at championship level with some measure of success. If you were to contemplate breeding from a dog of inferior quality, not only would that be unfair on the future of the breed, but you would be unlikely to produce stock of consistently high quality so that you achieve your aim of winning in the showring. Indeed you would hopefully have chosen a male with attributes that would improve the less good qualities in your own bitch, and you may just be lucky enough to produce something rather good, but that is not a sensible way to begin your breeding programme.

If your first dog is a male and he is not winning well in the ring, he is certainly not good enough to use at stud. There are many, many good dogs out there, so no breeder worth their salt is likely to want to use a not-so-good specimen on a quality bitch. There may indeed be the owner of a pet bitch living locally who thinks it would be a good idea to use your own dog at stud; they may indeed even offer you a puppy from the litter in lieu of payment. In a word, please don't do it, for the quality will be less than good and it is highly unlikely that the puppy you have back will be sufficiently good for the showring.

Looking at it from a more positive aspect, supposing that your first show dog, a bitch shall we say, has won well in the ring and you decide to have a litter from her. This seems like a good idea and may well be just the right thing to do provided that you choose the sire very carefully. Your bitch must be at least eighteen months old when she whelps her litter and will probably be a little older than that. This will depend to a large extent on the breed, but between two and four years of age is usually considered fairly safe for a bitch's first litter. Although this may sound like a great idea, if you don't already have another show dog you will have nothing to show for a good few months, maybe even a year or more if you have a coated breed. Although regrettably some people do so, you should not

A judge from Sweden assesses a Skye Terrier at a prestigious event in Scotland.

show a bitch in whelp because you would be exposing her to infection. After the litter has been born she will be bringing up her puppies for a few weeks, so will not be in good bodily condition for quite a while, and if she has a coat it may take months to grow it back again fully depending on her hormones and how much the youngsters succeeded in ruining her coat! While she is out of the ring and you are waiting for the puppy you have retained to be old enough to show, you will only be able to gaze at the ring from the perimeter, and is this really what you want to be doing?

So you will see that the chances are you will end up buying your second show dog too, but this time you will be better experienced and will have more knowledge upon which to draw. You will have had the opportunity to watch and to learn, will have seen stock in the ring that you admire and will have got some impression as to which breeders are the better ones. If you are lucky, and if they can see that you are genuine about wanting to show seriously at top level, they may just decide to let you have something good.

Should I stay with this breed, or go for another?

You should never allow anything to detract from your first show dog, whatever his faults. Through him you will have been introduced to the world of dogs and so you have a great deal to thank him for. Hopefully you will allow him to live out the rest of his life with you, either as a show dog or as a pet. You owe him that.

With a little experience behind you, you will now be in a better position to understand the pros and cons of your chosen breed. Doubtless you had good reason for selecting that breed in the first place and hopefully you will decide to pursue your interest further, staying with the same breed. However, maybe you have seen pitfalls that you didn't recognise before. Perhaps one of the most obvious drawbacks that newcomers find it difficult to come to terms with is the numerical strength of the breed they have chosen. Clearly, although you will still need to get past top winning dogs to win high honours, it is much easier to get a place in a small class of

Maybe you will decide to have a breed that is small enough to tuck comfortably under your arm, like this little Chihuahua.

The Eurasier is a relatively new breed. This one waits patiently in its crate for exhibition at an FCI show in Luxembourg. (CUNLIFFE)

dogs than it is in a big one. The strength of a breed, in numerical terms, varies from year to year, but it is not at all unknown to have upwards of thirty or forty exhibits in one class in some breeds. If this is the case, maybe you will decide to look for another breed as an alternative. Perhaps you will go for something similar, within the same Group, but with considerably lower entries at shows. Indeed some very experienced exhibitors campaign more than one breed, often one that attracts high entries at shows and another in which the entries are smaller. Having said that, what should really matter is whether or not you love the breed and feel that it is really the breed for you, fitting in with your personal lifestyle.

You may have made the error of having initially chosen a breed that is too large for you to handle successfully. You may have selected a Greyhound, only later to find that you are physically not able to do it justice in the ring; maybe you are unable to move it at the correct speed to show off its movement to best advantage. In this case maybe you should consider a Whippet, though offset against that you will have to contend with many more Whippets in the ring than Greyhounds!

Another thing you may have now discovered is that your chosen breed needs more attention paying to the coat than you were prepared for. If you have a heavy workload you may simply not find the time to bath and groom your dog fully every week, or even every four or five days. If that is the amount of care your dog needs to grow a spectacular coat you will never be able to present your dog to such a high standard that he will win top awards. In such a case you may again wish to consider changing breeds. If an Afghan was your first choice, maybe you should consider a Saluki or even a Greyhound, or then you might prefer to go for something different entirely, even in a different Group.

These two winners of their Stakes classes show the considerable difference in size between a Whippet and an Italian Greyhound.

Temperament is another aspect of a breed that maybe you didn't consider sufficiently carefully before you purchased your first show dog. Of course every breed has its attributes, but undoubtedly some are easier to handle than others. If yours is a large, strong, guarding breed you will have to be sufficiently strong, both mentally and physically to handle it with full control. A breed that was originally created to guard a flock from predators, to survive on the icy tundra or to challenge other dogs in combat will still, of necessity, have something of its ancestry in its genetic make-up. Undoubtedly breeds have changed over time and most are now eminently suited to sharing people's homes and behaving politely in the showring, but just occasionally their original instincts will display themselves. This can perhaps be sparked off by another dog threatening them, or even by a judge who is too heavy handed. Other breeds may carry a trait of being 'aloof with strangers' which, although perfectly correct and typical of the breed, makes them more difficult to show than others. All these things can make showing a dog less than pleasurable, in which case maybe you need to look for another breed that you will be able to handle more easily.

That does not mean to say that you have to change from a giant breed to a Toy breed. In fact if you multiplied the physical size of some of the Toy breeds they would be extremely difficult to handle. Personally I can see virtue in every breed; some I like more than others but I can think of no breed with which I have no affinity at all. Only two dogs have attempted to bite me whilst I have been judging; I shall not mention their breeds by name but suffice it to say they were certainly not breeds that one immediately thinks of as difficult. On the other hand I have judged many of the large breeds that one thinks of as antagonistic and even in countries such as Russia, Kazakhstan and Latvia, where many of the breeds shown in the Working Group are actually dogs that do an efficient job of work, I have never been challenged. That is not to say that judges should not be on their guard at all times, but I think all of us would agree that whether or not a dog is temperamentally suitable for the showring depends to a very large extent on the way it is trained and handled.

Many of the larger breeds are exceptionally docile, so if you really feel that you are not capable of controlling the breed that originally took your fancy, you do not necessarily

There are many differences between shows in Britain and in mainland Europe. A very obvious difference is that some dogs on the Continent are shown with cropped ears, as can be seen here on this Briard. (CUNLIFFE)

have to scale down in size. If you do decide to change your breed, not only should you look at the general temperament and manageability of the breed, but also at the breeding lines behind the dogs you are considering purchasing. Don't just look at the sire and dam, but also look further behind. Some of them may still be in the showring, so you may have a chance to meet or at least observe them in person. If not, make enquiries of people within the breed, carefully sifting out myth from factual information.

Mary Ray is highly renowned for her expertise in training dogs for Heelwork to Music. Every year at Crufts she and her dogs put on a memorable performance to enormous applause.

So, maybe you will stay with the breed you have originally chosen, or maybe you will decide to change to another breed for show purposes, but you can be almost certain that you will always keep a very soft spot in your heart for your original favourite, whatever happens in the future.

At the very beginning of this chapter I mentioned that most new exhibitors only remain in the dog game for about five years, but of course there are others who remain involved in the show scene for a lifetime and often several generations of a family are involved. Children can take part in Junior Handling classes at shows from the age of six and there is of course no limit to the age at which a person can show a dog. As time progresses some exhibitors go on to become breeders and judges and some of these, because of their heavy judging schedules which involve many nights spent away from home, continue to enjoy being at dog shows and meeting numerous dogs without any longer having dogs of their own. At whatever level people are involved, there is something very special about dog showing and if you are interested enough to have read this book I have a sneaking suspicion that you are one of those people who will long surpass that five year average.

Things to Think About

Am I showing at the right level?

Is dog showing really for me?

Can I improve my handling skills?

How can I learn more about my breed?

Is this the breed for me?

Surely the world's most unusual and possibly the rarest breed is the Norwegian Lundehund, known also as the Puffin Dog. Amongst its many very special traits, which include six full toes on each foot and a neck that can bend back 180 degrees, it has tremendous flexibility in its front legs as pictured here. (CUNLIFFE)

CHAPTER 13

HELPFUL EXTRAS

As time goes on the language used within the dog showing world will become second nature, but for the first few months, or even years, some of the phrases and expressions you hear will simply not make much sense and you can very easily be misled, perhaps causing you to land yourself in embarrassing situations by having used something in entirely the wrong context.

Remember that, according to its breed, your tiny puppy may grow into something very large, as shown here by this Bloodhound bitch and her youngster.

Show-goers' colloquialisms

Let us therefore begin by looking at some showgoers' colloquialisms. If you read and inwardly digest the following list you will undoubtedly be better armed with your own vocabulary so that soon enough you will feel 'one of them'!

Big Green One Challenge Certificate (also known as a CC).
Bridesmaid Term used typically to describe a dog that wins several Reserve Challenge Certificates but not that all important Challenge Certificate. It can also relate to a dog that constantly wins second prize in its class, rather than first.
Can't get past It is often said that one 'can't get past' a particular dog, indicating that a dog is always winning and is seemingly impossible to beat.
Down the line Not placed first or second; used generally with reference to a Reserve or VHC placing or lower.
Facey/Face judging This indicates that a judge appears to be judging the people rather than the dogs, i.e. placing those exhibitors who have well-known faces. Whilst this does happen from time to time, it is always worth bearing in mind that often the well-known faces have a great deal of experience and probably do have the better dogs.
Free stand To show a dog in a standing position for the judge to see, but allowing the dog to walk naturally into that pose (often aided by baiting with a tit-bit) rather than by positioning the dog's legs etc. by hand.
Gained his crown/title Became a Champion.
Go over A judge 'goes over' a dog to assess how well he is constructed and how closely he resembles the description in his Breed Standard. In effect it means the actual placing of the hands on the dog for the purpose of assessment.
Good doer A dog that eats and thrives well.
In the cards Awarded one of the prizes in a class.
Judging the other end of the lead Apparently judging the handler rather than the dog.
Knocked A dog is placed lower than might have been expected, implying that other dogs of seemingly lesser quality gained higher placings.
Laying on of hands This is said of a judge who goes through the motions of going over a dog, but apparently does not feel the dog sufficiently well to assess structure.
Looking for his third Said of a dog that is hoping to win a third Challenge Certificate and therefore gain the title of Champion. (Note that a dog having gained a third CC has to await KC confirmation before using the title officially.)
Made up Became a champion.
New dog A dog that has not been assessed in a previous class by the judge who is officiating.
Pulled out Short-listed with a few others before the judge selects the final placings in the class. 'Pulled out but not placed' is commonly used to indicate that a judge did consider a dog further in a numerically strong class, but eventually did not award this dog a place.
Put through Generally used at Championship level to indicate the dog that has been declared Best of Breed and has therefore been 'put through' to the Group.
Put up Placed first. This can also be used in relation to the winner of the Challenge Certificate.

Reserve ticket Reserve Challenge Certificate (RCC). Note that this is entirely different from the Reserve placing in a class, which is fourth, and is a mistake commonly made by newer exhibitors.
Seen dog A dog that has already been assessed by a judge in a previous class.
Set up To present one's dog in a standing position for the judge to see.
Stack/stacked With the same meaning as to 'set up' but indicating that legs and possibly also tail and head are actually placed in position by the exhibitor.
Table dog A dog that is examined by the judge on the table rather than on the floor. Sometimes in an Any Variety class a judge will request that all 'table dogs' stand at the front of the line for assessment before the larger breeds.
Thrown out Unplaced in a class. 'Thrown out with the rubbish' is also frequently heard.
Thrown out in good company Indicating that although one's dog was not placed, there were also other good dogs in the same class that were not awarded a placing.
Ticket Challenge Certificate.

Canine terms and terminology

Canine terminology is a veritable minefield, especially as many terms used by exhibitors and breeders vary from one breed to another and certain terminology can be fairly specific to a particular breed. For example in Poodles the colour 'brown' is used, whilst the very same colour is described as 'chocolate' in another. However, much of the terminology is universal and the KC's *Glossary of Canine Terms*, mentioned earlier, is an accurate and comprehensive guide.

The following will hopefully be of particular assistance to the relative newcomer.

Action The gait or movement of a dog. The way it walks, trots or runs.
Affix The registered name granted by the KC to breeders, upon payment of a fee. Also referred to as a prefix.
Anal glands Two small glands located one each side of the anus, just inside the anal sphincter and functioning as storage chambers for a secretion. (If a dog habitually scrapes its bottom along the ground, it may indicate that the anal glands need to be emptied, something that should be done by a vet unless you have been shown exactly how to do it yourself.)
Angulation Term used with reference to the various angles formed at a joint by the meeting of different bones. The degree of angulation required varies from breed to breed, such as the hind angulation of a German Shepherd Dog (Alsatian) showing a marked difference from that of the Chow Chow for example.
Apish Having a monkey-like expression.
Apple-headed A very domed, rounded skull, such as in the Chihuahua.
Balance A pleasing, well-proportioned blend of a dog's various features resulting in harmonious symmetry. The term can also be used for separate parts; balance of head; balance of body.
Barrel ribs Ribs beginning to arch outward as soon as they leave the vertebral column, thus giving a barrel shape to the chest. This is a fault in some breeds, but may be a character of other breeds.

Basset Hounds from this successful kennel are always presented to perfection.

Bat ear An erect ear that is broad at the base and rounded at the top, with its opening facing directly to the front.
Beard The thick long hair of muzzle and underjaw of some breeds.
Bitch A female.
Bitchy A male dog that looks feminine.
Bite The position of the upper and lower teeth in relation to each other when the mouth is closed.
Blaze A white marking running up the centre line of the face or forehead.
Bloom The sheen on a coat that is in prime condition.
Blown A coat that is moulting or casting.
Blue Colour used for a dog that is blue-grey in appearance. It is actually a dilution of a black coat colour and is perfectly acceptable in some breeds such as the Kerry Blue Terrier for example.
Bobtail A tail that has been docked to a very short length or a naturally tail-less dog. Also a commonly used word for the Old English Sheepdog.
Bone Used in connection with substance of bone and with particular reference to the girth of a dog's leg bones.
Brace Two dogs of the same kind. A Brace class is judged on the similarity of the brace or pair of dogs being exhibited.
Breeching The hair on the outside of the thighs and the back of the buttocks.
Breed characteristics The features of a breed that distinguish a dog as being typical of its breed.
Breed Standard The description of the ideal specimen of each breed.
Breeder/Br. The person who technically owns a bitch at the time of whelping (or the person to whom the dam was leased for the purpose). This means that someone who whelps a litter, if not the owner of the bitch, is not the breeder.
Brindle A colour pattern usually giving an almost striped effect, due to a mixture of black hairs with hairs of a lighter colour.
Brisket The forepart of the body that is below the chest and between the forelegs.
Broken coat A term used to describe a crinkly, harsh and wiry coat.
Broken colour A coat pattern in which the main colour is broken by white or another colour.
Brood bitch A bitch kept primarily for breeding purposes, often after her show career is over.
Brush A bushy tail, heavy with hair.
Butterfly nose A dark nose in which the pigment is broken by spotting of a flesh colour.
Button ear An ear in which the flap folds forward, the tip lying close to the skull, covering the opening and pointing forward.
Canines These are the four 'fang' teeth located at the outer edge of each row of incisors. They are the longest and strongest teeth in a dog's mouth.
Cat foot A round, compact foot with well arched toes, resembling that of a cat.
Chest The forepart of the body that is enclosed by the ribs.
China eye A clear blue eye.
Chiselling Clean cut lines and contours, especially on the face.
Clean neck Tight fitting skin around the neck, without loose skin, wrinkles or dewlap.

Cloddy Denoting a thick, heavy-set build.
Cobby Of compact conformation. Short-bodied.
Compact The union of various parts of the body that are closely put together. (Not rangy.)
Condition Denoting the overall fitness and health of the dog, as seen in body, coat, general appearance and deportment.
Conformation The various parts of the dog assembled together. Its form and structure.
Congenital Describing a feature (usually with reference to a defect) that is present at birth, as opposed to one developing later in a dog's life.
Couple Two hounds.
Coupling That part of the body located between the ribs and the pelvis.
Cow hocked Hocks turning inwards toward each other.
Crabbing Movement resembling that of a crab, with the hind feet moving out of parallel with the forefeet.
Crest The top part of the arch in a dog's neck. Crest can also denote full or sparse hair starting at the top of the head and tapering off down the neck.
Cropped ears The practice of cutting ears to make them stand erect. Crop-eared dogs may not be exhibited at shows in the UK.
Croup The area of the back from the front of the pelvis to the root of the tail.
Cryptorchid A male dog in which either one or both of the testicles have not descended into the scrotum. A bilateral cryptorchid is one in which neither testicle is descended, whilst in a unilateral cryptorchid only one side is affected. (See also *Monorchid* for comparison.)
Cushion The thick part of the upper lip, giving the impression of fullness.
Dewclaw The fifth digit on the inside of the legs. (Not always present on the hind legs.)
Dewlap Pendulous, loose skin under the throat.
Dish-faced A foreface in which there is a dip in the nasal bone so that the tip of the nose is higher than the stop. It can also denote a slight concavity in the nasal bone.
Dock Shortening the length of a dog's tail by cutting.
Double coat Two types of coat on one dog, namely an outer coat that is weather resistant and an undercoat for warmth and waterproofing.
Double handling Communication with an exhibit by another person outside the ring. (Something strictly against English KC rules.)
Down-faced The muzzle inclining downwards in an unbroken outward arc from the top of the skull to the tip of the nose.
Down at pastern A dog with weak or faulty pasterns that slope at a greater angle than is desirable from the vertical.
Drive Hindquarter propulsion; a powerful thrusting action.
Drop-eared Having ears hanging down close and flat to the side of the skull.
Dudley nose A brown, liver or putty coloured nose. Also sometimes called a putty nose.
East-west front Front feet turning outwards rather than facing straight forward.
Ectropion Eyelids turning outwards.
Entire A male dog with two normal testicles fully descended into the scrotum.
Entropion Eyelids turning inwards, frequently causing irritation because the eyelashes come into contact with the eyeball.

This lovely Yorkshire Terrier was brought over from Italy to compete at Crufts, gaining Best of Breed and later second in the Toy Group under one of the world's best-known judges, Terry Thorn.

Ewe neck The topline of the neck is concave; an anatomical weakness.
Fallaway The slope of the croup.
Feathering Long fringes of hair on ears, legs, tail or body.
Felted Having a matted coat.
Flag A feathered tail, as in Setters and Retrievers.
Flecked A coat that is just lightly ticked with another colour, but not roan or spotted. This can also be used to describe a flaw in a dog's normal eye colour.
Flews Pendulous corners of the lips of the upper jaw.
Floating rib The last or thirteenth rib, unattached to other ribs.
Flying ears Ears tending to fly out in opposite directions, or stand out further from the face than is expected in the breed.
Forearm The area from the elbow to the wrist.
Foreface The front part of the head, i.e. in front of the eyes.
Forehand/forequarters The whole of the front assembly from the shoulders right down to the feet and including the forelegs, forelimbs and thoracic limbs.
Foreleg Front leg from elbow to foot.
Free action Uninhibited free movement.
Frill Long hair on front of neck and forechest. Also called apron.
Furnishings An abundance of longer hair on head, legs, breechings and tail of some breeds.
Furrow A slight groove running down the centre of the skull.
Gait Pattern of footsteps at different rates of a dog's speed.
Gallop The fastest movement of a dog in which he is fully suspended in the air once during each sequence of the motion.
Gay tail A tail carried very high over a dog's back. Used frequently when a tail is carried higher than is desired within that breed.
Grizzle A mixture of colours, including bluish-grey, red and black.
Guard hairs Stiffer, usually longer hairs that serve as an outer jacket and protect the soft undercoat.
Hackney gait High lifting of the front feet. Generally a fault but correct in some breeds such as the Miniature Pinscher.
Hare foot A long narrow foot resembling that of the hare.
Harlequin Patched or pied colour as in some Great Danes. Usually black on white or blue on white.
Heart room Indicating ample room inside the chest cavity to allow heart development and function.
Heat A common term for a bitch's season or oestrus.
Height The height of a dog as measured from withers to ground when the dog is in a normal stance.
Hindquarters The rear part of a dog from the loin, including the feet.
Hip dysplasia A developmental disease of the hip joint in which the head of the femur (thigh bone) does not fit correctly into the socket of the pelvis.
Hock The collection of bones of the hind leg, forming the joint between the rear pastern and the lower thigh.

In-breeding The mating of closely related dogs, i.e. father/daughter; mother/son; brother/sister.
Incisors The upper and lower front teeth located between the canines.
Isabella A fawn colour, sometimes also described as a light bay.
Jowls The flesh of lips and jaws, often used in relation to heavy pendulous lips.
Keel Breastbone or sternum.
Knee joint Stifle joint.
Knitting An unsound crossing gait in which the elbows twist resulting in the legs criss-crossing and toeing out. Also known as weaving.
Knuckling over A weakness in the pastern joint causing the wrist to double forward while the dog is standing.
Layback The angle of the shoulder blade when viewed from the side. This term can also refer to the receding nose of the Bulldog.
Leather The upper flap of the ear. This expression is particularly in use in the Gundog breeds and with reference to the large hanging ears of some Hounds.
Leggy Too long in leg to give the correct balance for the breed.
Level back The line of the back running at a horizontal angle to the ground.
Level bite The upper and lower incisor teeth meet exactly edge to edge. Also called a pincer bite.
Line breeding The mating of dogs that are related, but not too closely so, such as those with a common grandparent.
Lippy Excessively pendulous lips, or lips that do not fit tightly.
Litter mates Dogs that were born in the same litter.
Liver A light brown colour, carrying no trace of black pigmentation.
Loin The area of the body on either side of the vertebral column, from the end of the ribcage to the start of the pelvis.
Low set Term used when the tail is set on below the level of the topline, or for ears that are set low. Low set can also indicate the short distance from the underline to the ground, especially in relation to overall height at withers, such as in the Basset Hound and Dachshund.
Lower thigh The area of the hindquarter from the stifle to the hock. Also known as second thigh.
Maiden bitch A bitch that has not produced puppies (This has no connection with the Maiden class at shows.)
Mane Long, profuse hair (often of a coarser texture than the rest of the coat) on the top and sides of the neck.
Mask Dark shading on the foreface, forming a mask-like pattern.
Merle A coat colouration of irregular dark blotches against a lighter background; usually blue-grey with flecks of black.
Mis-marked Of a colour contrary to that set down in the Breed Standard.
Molars The two back teeth on each side of the upper jaw and three back teeth on either side of the lower jaw.
Molera An opening in the top part of the skull, covered only by skin and hair. This is a special feature of some Chihuahuas.

Monorchid A male dog in which only one testicle has developed. (Not a unilateral cryptorchid.)
Moult Casting of the coat.
Moving close The hind legs moving close to each other.
Muzzle The front portion of the head between the stop and the tip of the nose; to include both upper and lower jaws.
N.A.F. Name applied for.
N.F.C. Not for competition.
Occiput The prominent bone found at the back point of the skull.
Outcrossing Breeding from a dog and bitch that have no common ancestors, at least in the first five generations.
Officers People who have been elected to hold office within a club or society.
Open coat A coat that is sparse, lacking in density.
Otter tail A thick tail, tapering to a blunt end. Short thick hair grows around the tail, which does not extend below the hock.
Out of coat A term used to describe a dog that has dropped its coat, usually temporarily, as in a moult.
Over-reaching Caused by more angulation and drive from the hindquarters than from the front, the hind feet step to one side of the front ones to avoid interference; they pass the front feet before making contact with the ground.
Overshot The incisors of the upper jaw overlap without touching the lower incisors when the mouth is closed.
Pacing Movement in which the two right feet move forward together, followed by the two left ones. Some dogs tend to pace when walking at a slow speed.
Pad The thickened portion of the sole of a dog's foot.
Paddling Movement in which the front feet make a circular motion, flicking outwards at the end of each step.
Particolour A coat of two colours, more or less equal in proportion. One of the two colours must be white.
Pastern The area between the wrist and the foot.
Pencilling Black line on the toes of some breeds.
Pied A coat of two colours in unequal proportions, one of the colours being white.
Pigment Depth and intensity of colour of skin and other tissues.
Pincer bite See *Level bite.*
Pips Name used for spots above the eyes of some black and tan dogs.
Plaiting See *Knitting.*
Plume A long fringe of hair on the tail.
Point of shoulder The foremost point of the shoulder blade (scapula), where it meets the upper arm.
Pompom Rounded tuft of hair left on the end of the tail when the coat has been clipped, as in the Poodle.
Pot-hook tail A tail carried above the back-line in an arc, without touching the back.
Prefix See *Affix.*
Premolars Four teeth (sixteen in all) on each side of the upper and lower jaws, located behind the canines and in front of the molars.

Prick ears Stiff, upstanding ears, usually with a pointed tip.
Queen Anne Front The forelegs are out at elbow, the pasterns close and the feet turned outward. Also known as a Chippendale Front.
Reach The distance covered by each stride when in motion.
Reachy Describing a dog with a long neck.
Reverse scissor bite The teeth of the lower jaw extending beyond those of the upper jaw, so that the front of the upper incisors meet with the back of the lower ones.
Ribbed up Ribs extending well back along the body.
Ring tail A long tail carried up and around, ending almost in a circle.
Roach A roached back is arched convexly along the spine, toward the loin.
Roan A uniform mixture of coloured and white hairs.
Rolling gait Characteristic rolling, ambling action in movement of breeds such as the Pekingese.
Rudder A term used for the tail, especially with reference to water dogs.
Ruff Thick, long hair around the whole of the neck area.
Run on To retain a puppy in the hope that it will turn out well enough for the purpose one has in mind, usually the showring.
Runt Usually used in connection with young puppies that are weedy, weak or undersized.
Sable A colour produced by black-tipped hairs on the background of another colour, the basic coat being gold, silver, grey, fawn or tan.
Saddle Coat of a different colour or quality over the back, in the shape of a saddle, as in the Afghan for example.
Scissor bite Upper incisors closely overlap the lower incisors so that the inside of the upper ones touch the outside of the bottom ones. Set square to the jaws.
Scrambled mouth Teeth not all set in a straight line, often seen in a narrow jaw. Also called a jumbled mouth.
Screw tail A tail that is naturally short and twisted more or less in a spiral.
Scrotum The scrotal sac containing the testicles of a male.
Second mouth The second set of teeth, i.e. the permanent set that replaces the milk teeth.
Second thigh The area of the hindquarters from the stifle to hock. Also called lower thigh.
Self coloured One solid colour all over.
Set on Term used to describe the place at which the ear meets the skull and that at which the tail meets the rump.
Shawl See *Mane/Ruff*.
Shelly Having a narrow, somewhat weedy body.
Shelly bone Porous, thin bone that is lacking in strength.
Shoulder height The height of a dog's body, measured from withers to ground.
Sickle hocked Refers to the shape and contours of the components of the hock joint. In profile the lower thigh and hind pastern from the shape of a sickle.
Single coat Many breeds have an outer coat and an undercoat and are thus 'double-coated'. A single-coated dog has only one coat, like an Italian Greyhound or Pointer.
Single tracking Convergence of the pads to a central line when in motion. This is a natural movement for longer-legged breeds.
Skully Thick and coarse in the skull.

Slab-sided Ribs that are too flat, lacking in spring from the spinal column. Also called herring gutted.
Snatching hocks A faulty gait which causes a noticeable rocking action in the hindquarters. The hock snatches outward as it passes the supporting leg, twisting the pastern in beneath the body.
Snipy A pointed weak muzzle that is too long and too narrow.
Socks The hair on the feet up to the pasterns; usually with reference to a different coat colour from the rest of the leg.
Soundness Quality of a dog that is well constructed throughout. A dog can also be described as being sound in temperament, meaning it has a good temperament.
Spectacles Light or dark markings around or over the eyes, or from the eyes to the ears.
Spayed A bitch that has had surgery to prevent her from having puppies.
Splay feet Toes set far apart from one another, irrespective of foot shape. Also termed open feet or open toed.
Spring of rib The amount of curvature of the rib cage.
Stand off coat Hair standing out from the body as opposed to lying flat to the skin.
Staring coat Hair that is out of condition; dry, harsh and open.
Steel blue A dark grey/blue colour, not silvery.
Steep Used to indicate insufficient angulation, especially in relation to shoulder and upper arm.
Stifle The knee joint of the hind leg, between the upper and lower thighs.
Stilted gait Jerking movement, caused by inflexible joints.
Stop The depression in the head, almost centrally between the eyes, where the nasal bone and skull meet.
Stud dog A male dog used to mate bitches.
Substance Indicating correct muscularity, condition and solidity.
Suffix An affix used at the end of the name (usually denoting the kennel name of the owner).
Sway back A back that sags concavely somewhere between the withers and hip bones.
T.A.F. Transfer applied for (to the KC).
Tail carriage The manner in which the tail is carried.
Tail set The position of the tail as set onto the croup.
Team Three or more exhibits of either sex.
Terrier front A front assembly that is straight and narrow.
Thick set Of broad and solid build.
Third eyelid Located in the inner corner of the eye is the third eyelid, a membrane used by the dog as a protective cover.
Throatiness Too much loose skin around the throat.
Ticking Small dark flecks of colour on a white ground.
Tie The locking together of a dog and bitch during mating.
Tied at elbow The elbows are set too close under the body, thereby restricting movement.
Toeing in Forefeet point in toward each other. This term can be used for dogs standing or on the move.
Topknot Tuft of long hair on top of the head of some breeds. The texture of the topknot varies according to the breed.

Winning high honours can be a tremendous thrill both for dog and owner, as clearly depicted here by Liz Waters with her Irish Water Spaniel.

Topline The outline of the dog from behind the withers to set on of tail.
Trace A dark mark down the back of a Pug.
Tri-colour A coat of three colours; black, white and tan.
Trousers Long or longish hair at the back of the legs of some breeds.
True movement Indicates that the feet and legs move in correct alignment.
Tuck up The underline of the abdomen as it sweeps up toward the flank; i.e. from end of rib to waist.
Tulip ears Ears that are wide and carried with a slight forward curve.
Type Characteristic qualities that distinguish a breed.
Undercoat Soft, often dense hair under the longer outer hair on some breeds.
Undershot Having lower incisor teeth protruding beyond the upper incisors so that they do not meet each other when the mouth is closed.

Upper arm The bone of the foreleg (humerus) below the shoulder blade and above the elbow.
Upright shoulder A lack of sufficient angulation in the shoulder blades.
Unsound A dog which, for physical or mental reasons, is incapable of carrying out the functional role of the breed.
Veil Long hair falling down over the eyes, as in the Skye Terrier.
Wall eye Eyes that appear white and blue (due to incomplete distribution of melanin deposits), as seen in breeds carrying the merle colour.
Weaving See *Knitting*.
Weedy Too lightly framed with inadequate bone. Lacking in substance.
Well sprung ribs See *Spring of rib*.
Wheaten Pale yellow or fawn colour. Can also be called straw.
Wheel back The back being markedly arched over the loin. Excessively roached.
Whelp A puppy from the time of birth until it is weaned.
Whelping The act of a bitch giving birth to puppies.
Whip tail A tail that is carried out straight, tapering to the end.
Whiskers Longer hair found on the muzzle sides and underjaw.
Winter nose A nose that is poorly pigmented, strictly speaking in the winter months.
Wirehaired A harsh, crisp coat of wiry texture, as found in many Terriers.
Withers The region of union between the uppermost portion of the shoulder blades and the first and second thoracic vertebrae; immediately behind the neck.
Wrinkle Loose folds of skin, primarily on the head and neck, but sometimes also on the body, as on the Shar-Pei.
Wry mouth The lower jaw is twisted to one side so that the upper and lower jaws are out of alignment with one another.
Zygomatic arch The bony ridge that forms the lower border of the eye socket, extending to the base of ear.

CHAPTER 14

THE SHOW SYSTEM ABROAD

Although the aim of any exhibitor is to win well or at least to gain a place in a class, the system of judging varies quite considerably from country to country, although there are of course many similarities too. In Britain shows are held under the auspices of the Kennel Club, but the two other main governing bodies in the canine world are the American Kennel Club (AKC) and Fédération Cynologique Internationale (FCI).

AKC

The AKC is the main governing body in the USA and was established in 1884, with the aim of promoting the study, breeding, exhibiting and advancement of pure-bred dogs. It became the registering body for all pure-bred dogs in the USA and is the largest, non-profit, pure-bred dog registry in that country. There are around five hundred independent dog clubs within the AKC and well over four thousand affiliate clubs, each of which follows AKC rules. Over one million dogs are registered each year, each of which belongs to a recognised AKC breed, of which there are about one hundred and fifty.

To hold an AKC registration number giving a dog the right to compete in AKC events, it must be of a recognised AKC breed. There are of course many other breeds in the USA, but if not AKC registered they operate under the auspices of different societies and breed clubs.

At AKC shows, as in Britain, dogs are always judged before bitches. There is less variety in the classes on offer, usually with six for each sex for non-champions (seven if the puppy class is divided into two by age). The classes are Puppy, for dogs between six and twelve months of age; a class for twelve to eighteen month old dogs; Novice, for dogs that have never won a first prize; Bred by Exhibitor; American-bred, for dogs that were born in the USA and Open, for all dogs and bitches. The winners from each of these classes then compete together in what is known as the Winners Class for each sex. The Winning dog and bitch then both compete against any Champions entered and for BOB, Best Opposite Sex also being declared. The BOB winner then goes on to compete against the other BOB winners within that Group.

As in Britain there are seven Groups, but in this case they are called Sporting Dogs, Hounds, Working Dogs, Terriers, Toys, Non-Sporting Dogs and Herding Dogs.

From the Winners Dog and Winners Bitch competition only, one dog and one bitch can win Championship points within their breed at each show, but there must be a sufficient number of entries. To gain the title of Champion, fifteen points are needed. Two major wins are required under different judges, these with a minimum of three and a

At shows abroad it is not unusual to see native breeds handled by owners in national costume, as here where this magnificent Komondor is being shown at the World Dog Show in Budapest, Hungary. (CUNLIFFE)

Presenting a top quality dog to absolute perfection can lead to winning top honours at a show. This American-bred Bichon Frisé is an American and an English Champion, handled by Michael Coad, one of this highly successful dog's co-owners.

maximum of five points. It is the number of dogs of each sex entered in the breed that determines how many points are awarded.

In the USA ribbons are given in each class; blue is first, red is second, yellow third and white fourth. For BOB a purple and gold ribbon is presented, whilst Best of Winners, this being the better of the Winners Dog (best male) and Winners Bitch (best female), receives a blue and white ribbon. Best Opposite Sex receives a red and white one, so colours are significant and the ultimate winner of Best in Show wins a red white and blue rosette.

The various AKC titles can be mind-boggling to the outsider, for there are over forty of them. Champion, abbreviated as Ch is perhaps universal but many American dogs have a string of titles used as suffixes such as CD (Companion Dog), MX (Master Agility Excellent), JE (Junior Earthdog), OTCH (Obedience Trial Champion), CT (Champion Tracker), FC (Field Champion) etc. The list seems endless! Indeed in America there is plenty of opportunity for show dogs to compete in other sports too and as in the UK, there is a Canine Good Citizen Program for those want to teach their dogs the best of manners so that they are true canine companions.

FCI

The FCI was established in 1911 with Germany, Austria, Belgium, France and the Netherlands as the founding nations. Sadly the First World War brought things to a halt, but it was recreated in 1921 by the Société Centrale Canine de France and the Société Royale Saint-Hubert in Belgium, where the FCI offices are still situated in Thuin. Now there are as many as eighty member countries; each of which trains its own judges.

Many more breeds are recognised by the FCI than by the AKC and English KC, the figure being around three hundred and thirty. Each breed is considered the property of a particular country and individual countries are responsible for writing the breed standards for their national breeds, in conjunction with the FCI's Standards and Scientific Commissions. These standards are published in four languages, English, French, German and Spanish, these being the four official languages of the FCI.

Although the FCI issues rules and regulations for International Shows, each member country has its own rules with the result that although all FCI shows are similar, they are by no means identical. Although in Britain and the USA judges are well used to judging many more dogs in a day, at an FCI show a judge rarely officiates for more than ninety. This is partly because each dog receives a critique on the day, whereas in the UK the judge makes notes on only the first one, two, or possibly three placings, and this is published later so the notes need only be rough.

Another difference at FCI shows is that every dog is given a grading such as Sufficient (Suff), Good (G), Very Good (VG) or Excellent (Exc); Not Promising, Satisfactory, Promising or Very Promising in the case of puppies. Exhibits can also be Disqualified for their ill temper or aggressive behaviour, or for their serious lack of conformation to breed type. They can also be marked 'Cannot be judged', applicable if the dog fails to move or avoids examination, or if the judge suspects faking which has changed the dog's appearance.

The most prestigious FCI shows are the World Dog Show, held in a different country each year, Section Dog Shows which are the European, Asian and Americas/Caribbean, which again are hosted by different countries each year and International Championship

Shows. At these dogs can compete for a CACIB in each sex, this being the *Certificat d'Aptitude au Championnat Internationale de Beauté*, and at the former can gain the title of World Champion and for example European Champion. The CAC, a national title, is also awarded at these shows, as it is at other shows that do not hold international status. However, there are variations from country to country regarding from which classes dogs can compete for the national certificate. Reserve CACs and Reserve CACIBs are not awarded in every country.

The American Staffordshire Terrier is forbidden in some countries, but this youngster at a Luxembourg show has the sweetest temperament and was much admired by the author. (CUNLIFFE)

The classes are also different under the FCI system, with the Puppy Class being for puppies between the age of six and nine months only. Junior is for dogs between nine and eighteen months and there is an Intermediate class for which dogs between fifteen and twenty-four months are eligible. In the Open and Working classes dogs must be fifteen months or over, as they must in the Champion Class in which the exhibits must hold a national or international title. Some breeds need to have a Working Trial in order to earn the title of CACIB. Veteran classes under the FCI system are for dogs over eight years old, whereas in Britain dogs become veterans at seven.

There are ten different groups at FCI shows, making them very different from shows in Britain and America:

Group 1	Sheepdogs and Cattle Dogs (except Swiss Cattle Dogs)
Group 2	Pinschers, Schnauzers, Mastiffs (Molosser breeds) and Swiss Mountain and Cattle Dogs and Other breeds
Group 3	Terriers
Group 4	Dachshunds (Teckels)
Group 5	Spitz and Primitive types
Group 6	Scenthounds and related breeds
Group 7	Pointing Dogs
Group 8	Retrievers, Flushing Dogs and Water Dogs
Group 9	Companion and Toy Dogs
Group 10	Sighthounds

Judging abroad is something that this book's author thoroughly enjoys, for it affords her the opportunity of assessing the standard of dogs in so many countries. Here she is pictured with two excellent Tibetan Mastiffs to whom she awarded the CACIBs in Luxembourg. (ANON.)

Such is the international atmosphere of dog showing that this highly successful Hungarian Vizsla, Sh.Ch./Aust.Ch. Hungargunn Bear It'n Mind, was bred in Australia but came to the U.K. where he won many Best in Show awards.

Other shows

Several countries hold shows other than those under the auspices of the FCI, so that in some countries there are two or more kennel clubs operating under differing systems. In some cases the clubs work together amicably, but sadly this is not always the case. In some countries, such as in Russia, certain breeds of dog do not fall into the categories of breeds registered under the FCI system, so their owners can only exhibit them at alternative shows.

In Southern Ireland the Irish Kennel Club (IKC) is very active. Here dogs can become Irish Champions under the country's own Green Star system, but the IKC now holds FCI shows too.

APPENDIX 1

Useful contacts

Our Dogs
5 Oxford Road Station Approach
Manchester
M60 1SX
Telephone: 0870 0624062
Fax: 0870 7316699

Dog World
Somerfield House
Wotton Road
Ashford
Kent
TN23 6LW
Telephone: 01233 621877
Fax: 01233 645669

The Kennel Club
1-5 Clarges Street
Piccadilly
London WIY 8AB
Telephones:
Customer Services: 0870 606 6750
Petlog: 0870 606 6751
Library/Gallery: 020 7518 1009
Insurance Enquiries: 01296 390617

The Irish Kennel Club
Fottrell House
Harolds X Bridge
Dublin 6W
IRELAND
Telephone: Int + 353 (1) 4533300
Fax: Int + 353 (1) 4533237

FCI Office
Place Albert 1er, 13
B-6530 Thuin
BELGIUM
Telephone: Int + 32.71.59.12.38
Fax: Int + 32.71.59.22.29
E-mail: info@fci.be

AKC
Headquarters
260 Madison Ave
New York, NY 10016
Telephone: Int + 212 696 8200

Operations Center
5580 Centerview Drive
Raleigh, NC 27606
Telephone: Int + 919 233 9767

APPENDIX 2

SUGGESTED READING

As a dedicated dog owner and potential exhibitor, there will be a multitude of books available to read, but exactly what you should read will depend very much upon your breed.

Kennel Club Publications

Many KC publications are useful and a complete list can be obtained by contacting the Kennel Club at 1-5 Clarges Street, Piccadilly, London, W1J 8AB
Telephone: 0870 6066750
E-mail: info@the-kennel-club.org.uk
Internet: www.the-kennel-club.org.uk

Of particular interest will be the Breed Standards, which may be purchased on a 'per Group' basis without illustrations, or if you have a wider interest *The Kennel Club's Illustrated Breed Standards* is updated and published in 'coffee table' book form every few years. Breed Standards are also available for download from the Kennel Club's comprehensive web site.

Veterinary Books

There are several good veterinary books available, but those I keep on my own shelf are:

Veterinary Notes For Dog Owners, edited by Trevor Turner, published by Popular Dogs
Black's Veterinary Dictionary, edited by Geoffrey West, published by Adam and Charles Black

You will also be able to pick up much information about genetic problems that are specific to certain breeds in breed books, especially if they have been authored by a breed specialist. Genetic problems are also sometimes discussed in breed club publications, and there is a regular veterinary column in each of the two weekly canine newspapers.

Breed Club Publications

If you join one or more breed clubs specific to your chosen breed, it is likely that they will issue newsletters and probably a Year Book, all of which are likely to contain articles of interest, sometimes with guidance about showing topics and about grooming. In such publications you are also likely to see pictures of dogs belonging to other members of the club, helping you to 'get your eye in' on the breed.

Some breed clubs also publish extended Breed Standards which, if carefully compiled, can be very useful as an aid to better understanding of the conformation of your breed.

Breed Specific Books

Clearly it is important that you own a really in-depth book specific to your own particular breed. If carefully chosen, this will give you information not only about the history of the breed which will doubtless be of interest, but also sound advice as to care and grooming as applicable for this particular breed. As briefly mentioned above, it may also contain a chapter on health issues, which is sure to be useful in case problems arise during your dog's life.

Canine Journals

There are several monthly publications of the glossy variety and these can usually be found on the shelves at major retail outlets.

Important reading material for anyone involved in the dog showing world are either or both of the two following weekly canine newspapers:

Dog World, Somerfield House, Wotton Road, Ashford, Kent, TN23 6LW
Telephone: 01233 621877

Our Dogs, 5 Oxford Road Station Approach, Manchester, M60 1SX.
Telephone: 0870 0624062

INDEX